With over 1000 illustrations in color and black and white

THE JACKSONS LEGACY

by **THE JACKSONS** with **FRED BRONSON**

BLACK DOG
& LEVENTHAL
PUBLISHERS
NEW YORK

PAGES 4–5 Before famed Hollywood photographer Lawrence Schiller set up this session with the Jackson 5 on the beach in Malibu in 1969, he had taken photographs of dozens of celebrities, including Marilyn Monroe, Clint Eastwood, Barbra Streisand, Paul Newman, Bette Davis, Muhammad Ali, Robert Kennedy, and Richard Nixon.

PAGES 6–7 The 45 rpm 7-inch single was introduced by RCA on January 10, 1949. Before streaming, digital downloads, and CDs, record companies released millions of singles on vinyl, sometimes with "picture sleeves." This collection shows the international scope of the Jackson 5's releases, with different covers from all over the world.

PAGES 8–9 The dramatic opening of the 1984 *Victory* tour set the stage for one of the most successful, highest-grossing tours of all time. The fans who filled stadiums all over North America screamed as the Jacksons rose up from below the stage for their first song, "Wanna Be Startin' Somethin'."

CONTENTS.

"I'M VERY PROUD OF MY BOYS, EVEN BEFORE THEY BECAME THE JACKSON 5. JOE WOULD HAVE THEM REHEARSE AT LEAST THREE TIMES A WEEK. THE NEIGHBOURHOOD WOULD COME AROUND; THEY WOULD BE CROWDED AROUND THE WINDOW, AND IN THE YARD DANCING."

KATHERINE JACKSON

"THEY WERE WINNING ALL THE TALENT SHOWS IN THE STATE ... THEY COULD PERFORM WITH ANYBODY ANYWHERE, ALL OVER THE WORLD. AND WHEN IT CAME TO MOTOWN THEY HAD SOMETHING TO OFFER BERRY GORDY."

JOE JACKSON

"ONCE I SAW THEM I KNEW THAT THEY WERE MAGICAL AS A GROUP. THEN, I TOOK THEM TO CALIFORNIA AND THEY ENDED UP LIVING WITH ME ... I DIDN'T MIND THE NOISE. WE SANG AND WE PLAYED AND WE REHEARSED. WE HAD A LOT OF FUN. WE HAD BASEBALL GAMES EVERY WEEK—THE JACKSONS VERSUS THE GORDYS—AND WE WERE VICIOUS COMPETITORS. I WAS TRYING TO TEACH THEM THAT COMPETITION BREEDS CHAMPIONS, BUT YOU CAN'T LET THE COMPETITION GET IN THE WAY OF THE LOVE."

BERRY GORDY

2300 Jackson Street
Gary, Indiana

May 4, 1951
Jackie Jackson is born
to Joe and Katherine Jackson,
followed by...

October 15, 1953
...Tito Jackson

December 11, 1954
...Jermaine Jackson

March 12, 1957
...Marlon Jackson

January 31, 1968
Their disc debut, "Big Boy,"
is released on Steeltown
Records, Gary

March 5, 1968
"Big Boy" is reissued with
distribution by leading national
record label, Atco

July 12, 1968
At Chicago's Regal Theater, it's
a "Battle of the Groups" between
the Jackson Five, the Chi-Lites,
the Vibrations, and Bobby Taylor
& the Vancouvers, among others

July 23, 1968
Journeying from Gary to Detroit,
the group auditions at Motown, and
the videotape is sent to Berry Gordy
in Los Angeles

March 11, 1969
The Jackson 5 officially sign
to Motown Records

December 14, 1969
The group debuts on
The Ed Sullivan Show, CBS-TV

April 25, 1970
Dislodging the Beatles' "Let It Be,"
the group's electric "ABC" is
the brothers' second No. 1

June 20, 1970
The Jackson 5 sell out the
Los Angeles Forum, with more than
18,000 in attendance. The show is
recorded and eventually released
on album forty years later

June 27, 1970
"The Love You Save" is the five's
third consecutive *Billboard* Hot 100
No. 1, replacing the Beatles' "The
Long And Winding Road"

October 17, 1970
With "I'll Be There," the Jackson 5
become the first group in *Billboard*
Hot 100 history to reach No. 1 with
their first four charted singles

January 12, 1972
The group takes part in a
Martin Luther King birthday
commemorative concert at Atlanta's
Metropolitan Auditorium

June 30, 1972
As part of their US tour, the
Jackson 5 perform at Madison
Square Garden, New York

September 30, 1972
The Jackson 5 are among the acts
playing at the "Save The Children"
concert at PUSH Expo '72, Chicago

October 14, 1972
Michael's first solo No. 1 on
Billboard Hot 100 is "Ben," from
the movie of the same name

October 30, 1972
The Jackson 5 perform for, and
meet, Britain's Queen Mother at the
annual Royal Variety Performance
at the London Palladium

May 18, 1974
"Dancing Machine" is No. 2
on *Billboard* Hot 100, powered by
Michael's "robot" dance moves
on TV's *Soul Train*

August 3, 1974
The Jackson 5 return to No. 1
on the *Billboard* charts, singing
backup on Stevie Wonder's
"You Haven't Done Nothin'"

December 15, 1974
Jermaine marries Berry Gordy's
daughter, Hazel Joy, in Los Angeles,
where Smokey Robinson performs
a new song, "Starting Here And
Now," for the couple

February 15, 1975
The group opens for Bob Marley
& the Wailers at the National
Stadium, Kingston, Jamaica

February 13, 1976
During their tour of Asia,
the Jackson 5 play six concerts
in Manila, Philippines

September 3, 1980
The brothers are honored with
a star on the Hollywood Walk
of Fame as "The Jacksons"

November 8, 1980
Triumph enters the Top 10
of the *Billboard* album charts

July 8, 1981
The Jacksons' *Triumph* North
American tour opens in Memphis

November 30, 1982
Michael's *Thriller* is released
by Epic Records. It goes on to
become the most popular album
in history, with more than 100
million sales worldwide

February 26, 1983
Thriller is No. 1 on the *Billboard*
album charts for the first of its
record-breaking thirty-seven
weeks at the top

May 30, 1989
The group's last album
2300 Jackson St, named after
their original home in Gary,
is released by Epic Records

November 18, 1989
Jermaine's "Don't Take It Personal"
reaches No. 1 on the *Billboard*
Hot Black Singles chart

November 15, 1992
The Jacksons: An American Dream
two-part, five-hour mini-series
makes its debut, with record ratings
for the ABC-TV network

May 15, 1997
The brothers are inducted into
the Rock and Roll Hall of Fame
as the "Jackson Five"

September 7, 2001
The Jacksons reunite once more,
performing their Motown hits at
New York's Madison Square Garden
as part of a thirtieth anniversary
tribute to Michael's solo career

August 29, 1958
...Michael Jackson

October 29, 1961
...Randy Jackson

August 29, 1965
Billed as "The Jackson Five,"
the group performs at a back-to-
school "Jamboree" at the Big Top
shopping center, Gary

1966
The Jackson Five's first
professional – that is, paid – shows
take place at Mister Lucky's
Lounge in Gary

August 13, 1967
The brothers win first prize at
a talent contest at New York's
historic Apollo Theater

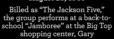

July 10, 1969
The group starts recording sessions
in Detroit with Bobby Taylor in the
producer's chair

July 1969
The brothers make California their
new home, and Berry Gordy assigns
Suzanne de Passe to mentor them

October 7, 1969
"I Want You Back," written and produced
by the Corporation, is the group's first
Motown release and becomes the five's
explosive first No. 1 on the
Billboard Hot 100

October 18, 1969
Diana Ross introduces the
Jackson 5 on ABC-TV's
nationwide *The Hollywood Palace*

December 12, 1969
Motown releases the album
Diana Ross Presents The Jackson 5

December 19, 1970
The Jackson 5's *Christmas Album*
and their "Santa Claus Is Coming
To Town" 45 are both No. 1 on the
Billboard Christmas charts

January 31, 1971
The group plays a benefit concert
for Gary mayor Richard Hatcher
at the West Side High School

September 11, 1971
Saturday cartoon series *Jackson
5ive* debuts on ABC-TV at 8:30am

September 19, 1971
The *Goin' Back To Indiana*
television special airs on ABC-TV
with guests Diana Ross, Bobby
Darin, and Bill Cosby

October 7, 1971
"Got To Be There" is Michael's first
solo single release, reaching No. 4
on the *Billboard* Hot 100

November 5, 1972
The Jackson Five Show debuts
on CBS-TV

November 1972
The group performs at Olympia
Music Hall, Paris, and Empire Pool,
Wembley, London

March 10, 1973
Jermaine's remake of "Daddy's
Home" hits the *Billboard* Top 10

April 30, 1973
The group performs concerts
in Japan, including an Osaka
show that is recorded and later
released on album

October 26, 1973
Jackie Jackson's solo LP
is released by Motown

March 1976
The group signs to Epic Records as
the Jacksons. Jermaine goes solo
and stays at Motown; Randy officially
joins the group's line-up

June 16, 1976
CBS-TV debuts *The Jacksons*
summertime television series

June 25, 1977
"Show You The Way To Go" tops the
British charts; it is the group's
first post-Motown No. 1

October 13, 1979
"Don't Stop 'Til You Get Enough"
becomes Michael's second solo
No. 1 on the *Billboard* Hot 100

May 17, 1980
Jermaine's "Let's Get Serious,"
cowritten and produced by Stevie
Wonder, is No. 1 on *Billboard*'s
Hot Soul Singles chart

May 16, 1983
The group reunites for NBC-TV's
Motown 25 special, and Michael's
"moonwalk" on the telecast is
seen by tens of millions

July 6, 1984
The Jacksons kick off their
Victory tour at Kansas City's
Arrowhead Stadium

August 4, 1984
Victory hits the Top 5 of the
Billboard album charts

January 28, 1985
Cowritten by Michael, USA For Africa's
"We Are The World" is recorded with
producer Quincy Jones at the A&M
Studios in Hollywood with various
Jacksons at the session

November 21, 1987
Marlon's "Don't Go" reaches
No. 2 on the *Billboard* Hot
Black Singles chart

June 25, 2009
Michael dies in Los Angeles

December 13, 2009
The Jacksons: A Family Dynasty
debuts on the A&E TV channel

June 20, 2012
The Jacksons begin their first group
tour without Michael, playing forty-
plus shows across North America,
Europe, Asia, and Australasia

June 2017
The Jacksons' fiftieth
anniversary tour begins

2300 JACKSON STREET.

IN GARY, INDIANA, JOE AND KATHERINE JACKSON RAISE THEIR NINE CHILDREN IN A SMALL TWO-BEDROOM HOME
FILLED WITH LOVE AND MUSIC. THE THREE OLDEST BROTHERS FORM A BAND, AND ARE EVENTUALLY JOINED BY TWO OF
THEIR YOUNGER BROTHERS. GLADYS KNIGHT SEES THEM PERFORM IN CHICAGO AND CALLS MOTOWN. SOON AFTER,
MOTOWN'S BOBBY TAYLOR TELLS THE COMPANY TO GIVE THE BOYS AN AUDITION.
IN MARCH 1969 BERRY GORDY SIGNS THE JACKSON 5.

AS A HIGH-SCHOOL student, Katherine Scruse and her friends organized house parties where they could meet boys and dance to the R&B songs that were popular on the radio—especially the slow ones. It was at one of these "blue light" socials that she first saw a handsome boy who took her breath away. His name was Joe Jackson, and not very long after that first meeting Joe took a bride—but it was not Katherine. She was disappointed, but not for long. A year later, Joe got a divorce and when he turned up at Katherine's door at Christmas time with a present, Katherine knew he was interested in her. They were married on November 5, 1949, in Crown Point, Indiana.

Joe was born in Arkansas and Katherine in Alabama. Both of their families moved to East Chicago, Indiana, where Joe found a job at the Inland Steel Company, working in the mill as a crane operator. As a couple, they dreamed of owning a home in California, and Joe promised Katherine they would live there one day. But as young newlyweds—Joe was twenty and Katherine nineteen—their budget permitted only a two-bedroom wood-frame house in Gary, Indiana. By coincidence, their new home was located at 2300 Jackson Street. They purchased it for $8,500 and borrowed $200 from Katherine's father to make the $500 down payment. Joe was bringing home only $56 a week from the mill, so the family did without a telephone and a TV at first, finally purchasing their first set in 1953. To stay warm on cold Indiana nights, the family would crowd into the kitchen and sit by the oven.

MARLON JACKSON: It was a tiny house, but it seemed huge to us while we were living there.

It truly was a small house, but it seemed like it would be big enough for the family they were planning. Joe wanted one child and Katherine thought they should have three. They had no idea they would raise nine children in this home. By the time they had a full house, Joe and Katherine slept in one bedroom, while their sons Jackie, Jermaine, Tito, Marlon, Michael, and Randy shared the other bedroom. The three Jackson daughters—Rebbie, LaToya, and Janet—slept on fold-out couches in the living room.

In his book *You Are Not Alone: Michael, Through a Brother's Eyes*, Jermaine wrote,

"We shared a metal-framed three-tiered bunk bed. Its length was just big enough to fit against the back wall and its height meant that Tito and I slept head to toe, about four feet from the ceiling. In the middle were Michael and Marlon, and Jackie had the lowest bunk all to himself. Jackie was the only brother who didn't know what it was like to wake up with a foot in his eyes, ear, or mouth."

JACKIE JACKSON: There was a lot of love in that little house. My mother was the sweetest woman you could ever meet. She acted more like a sister to us. My father was the one who cracked the whip; my mom was more easy-going. She worked at the Sears department store. I remember one time there was a blizzard and I was looking out of the window for her to come home, because I knew what time she finished work. I finally saw her from a distance, walking through the snow, and she slipped and fell. I ran to help her, with tears in my eyes. She did everything for us and has always been a great friend to this day. My father was strict because he had to be. Gary wasn't the safest place to live. There were gangs, and dad had six boys. He wanted to make sure we didn't get involved in any gangs or get into drugs, so he kept us busy.

MARLON: He would have us move bricks from one side of the backyard to the other. We'd stack them up on one side of the yard, and two days later he'd have us move them back. They weren't little bricks, and there was a lot of them. It was an all-day job, designed to keep us off the streets.

JACKIE: I thank him for making us do that. When I look back at moving those bricks, I realize what he was doing. A lot of the guys I grew up with are dead now. My father saw that we had talent and he got us out of a very rough environment.

TITO JACKSON: We were playing a local city auditorium and there were four guys who wanted to get in, so they decided to take the equipment from our hands and walk in with it like they were with us. My father didn't like it so he told them to give it back, but they wouldn't. They beat him up over it. I remember Michael running to the phone booth to call the police. They were big guys to us, because we were little kids. It was a difficult show to do because we knew our father was

headed off to the hospital and we still had to go on and sing. That was really bad.

Before his brothers were born, Jackie had one older sister: Maureen, known affectionately as Rebbie.

JACKIE: Rebbie was the overseer. She made sure that all of the children were taken care of. She was like a mother figure to the younger kids after they were born, and I was like a father figure. We did everything from washing the clothes and hanging them up to keeping the house clean. As a teenager, I felt more like an adult. I was like a counselor, keeping my brothers in line. When my mom and dad weren't there, it was up to me to oversee things. I felt like I couldn't be myself, or have a girlfriend. We were so busy making music that I didn't have a day free when I could take a girl out.

TITO: Being a kid in Gary was fun. We would shovel snow to make money. We cut lawns and pulled weeds. I helped my neighbor with his paper route, delivering newspapers on Mondays, Wednesdays, Fridays, and Sundays, then I got my own route. Jermaine would help me. We'd wake up in below-zero weather. There would be five stacks of newspapers that we had to fold and put in bags.

JERMAINE JACKSON: I call those days [in Gary] the best days, because I remember walking to the store with Tito, or going for a strawberry soda or a bag of potato chips. I remember running across the field, playing baseball. Those days we can never relive. Now I look back on them as something very, very special.

It wasn't all work. The boys found ways to entertain themselves, especially when their parents weren't home.

JACKIE: I loved having brothers. We played a lot of sports. When our parents left for work, we would move the furniture around and fight with boxing gloves. That was really a lot of fun. I'd win all the time, and then I'd remind everyone not to tell mom and dad. I even gave my younger brothers candy and made them promise not to say anything. Then as soon as my mom came home, the others would say, "Jackie's fighting!" She'd be very upset.

Boxing wasn't the only sport in which Jackie excelled.

JACKIE: There was a moment when I thought I was going to be a baseball player. We all played baseball back in the day, all my brothers. There was a baseball field right behind our home, not even forty yards away. I was a shortstop and a pitcher. I did pretty well for a little while, but music was something that I wanted really badly with my brothers. I used to watch the San Diego Chargers on TV, and I watched the Cleveland Browns and the Chicago Bears. It was Gale Sayers and Dick Butkus at the time. When I watched those games, it was cold and there was snow on the ground. And then the next game would show the San Diego Chargers in California. There would be palm trees on the TV and I would think, "Oh my God, how can I get there?" People in the stands would be enjoying the nice weather in January and we would be freezing. I played on local teams and in Babe Ruth leagues, but I wanted music more than baseball because I knew music was something you could sing forever. Baseball and other sports meant you'd have a short career. You could only play for so long. Scouts for the Chicago White Sox were watching me. Eventually I had to make a decision, and I chose music. I wanted to be with my brothers and they loved music so much. I was the oldest, and I thought if I wasn't with them, it might hurt the group, so I decided to make music with them and it was the right move.

The house on Jackson Street was filled with music, and not just from the family record collection or the radio. Joe and his brother Luther had a band, the Falcons.

JACKIE: We would watch them play music all the time. We were fascinated to see them play the blues and guitar. We could sit around for hours and hours just watching them play. We really looked up to my father and our uncle and their friends. That was how my brothers and I became interested in music.

In his book *You Are Not Alone: Michael, Through a Brother's Eyes,* Jermaine reminisced, "Uncle Luther played the blues and Joseph switched between his guitar and the harmonica. Those were the sounds that sometimes helped us drift off to sleep."

While Joe was passionate about the blues, Katherine grew up listening to country music. Her father loved to tune in to the *Grand Ole Opry* on the radio and he would play country songs on his box guitar while Katherine and her sister Hattie sang along.

TITO: Our mother would sing while she was washing the dishes or doing the laundry, and all of us kids would harmonize with her. We sang "Cottonfields" a lot.

MARLON: I remember singing Roger Miller's "King Of The Road"; that was another one of her favorite songs. We loved singing with our mother. She was the one who kept our house together while our father worked. She was a disciplinarian, but not as much as my father.

TITO: Watching the Falcons rehearse in the house, I used to stare at their guitars. I wasn't paying any attention to their vocals; I was only interested in the guitars. My father warned us not to touch his guitars while he was at work. "When I'm out, don't be fooling with my guitar," he'd tell us. My mother would let me know when dad was about to arrive home from work so I could put the guitar away before he found me playing it. Three or four months went by and I was playing songs like "Louie Louie." I tried to remember what he was doing with his hands and to copy that. He never knew I was playing his guitar until the day I broke one of the strings. I didn't know what to do, and my mother told me, "Don't worry, I'll talk to him." But I knew that wasn't going to be good enough. I knew my father and how angry he was going to be. He came home and went to play his guitar and saw the broken string. The first thing he said was, "Who's been playing my guitar?" I started crying and he gave me a good spanking. Then he told me to sit down and he said, "Show me what you know." I was playing the guitar and still crying, and he looked at my mother and said, "Kate, this one can play." She replied, "I told you so. You should listen. They sing a little bit, too." But he didn't have the time to listen to us; he was too busy working and he thought we were just kids fooling around. He didn't know Jackie, Jermaine, and I had been harmonizing with our mother. It was just the three of us at this point. Marlon and Michael were little babies. They wanted to play with their toys, so we would kick them out of the room while we played music. We were serious about what we were doing, but our father would tell us to be quiet because he was trying to sleep so he could get up early and go to work.

The boys' musical knowledge wasn't limited to the songs the Falcons played or the country songs their mother loved. They listened to the radio and visited their local record store, too.

JACKIE: We were buying 45s. We'd go to the store, and that's where we discovered Johnny Mathis. We'd see his albums on display and he was really elegant, so groomed with his hair. We'd stare at his album covers. We loved his songs like "Chances Are" and "Gina" and really looked up to him, as well as Mary Wells and later the Delfonics. We loved "Venus" by Frankie Avalon, too. Before gigs, we'd play those songs backstage, just for us. We still do that today—you'll hear us playing "Venus" before we go out. It's such a beautiful song.

It wasn't long before the three Jacksons expanded to five.

JACKIE: Tito, Jermaine, and I started the group. We were just fooling around on guitar and bass and then one day Michael joined us, playing bongos on a Quaker oatmeal box. He played them so well we thought he should be part of the group. As soon as we did that, he started dancing up in front, doing his James Brown thing. Michael always watched James Brown on television, and Jackie Wilson, too. Also the Temptations and the Four Tops. He would copy what they were doing. That's when we realized how much showmanship he had, and we thought maybe he should be up front, singing lead. Michael was a little kid at the time but he was very professional.

TITO: Michael and Marlon had both been asking to be in the group. We kept telling them they were too young, that this was just for their big brothers. When Michael was in first grade, he proved himself singing "Climb Ev'ry Mountain" from *The Sound of Music* at Garnett Elementary School. We told Michael, "You're in the band now." Then Marlon said, "Me, too?" We told him, "You too, Marlon."

In his autobiography *Moonwalk,* Michael described how he was overwhelmed at the ovation he received from the audience in the school auditorium. "The applause was thunderous and people were smiling; some of them were standing. My teachers were crying and I just couldn't believe it. I had made them all happy. It was such a great feeling. I was a little confused, too, because I didn't think I had done anything special. I was just singing the way I sang at home every night."

With the brothers now officially a quintet, word of their musical prowess spread through the neighborhood.

JACKIE: Whenever we played music at home, kids who lived nearby would gather outside and peek in the windows to watch us. We really enjoyed that, playing Motown songs and hits by Sam Cooke and Sam & Dave and all those musicians from Stax. We loved to play "Green Onions" by Booker T. & the M.G.'s. It was the best music. We were crazy about the Motown beat and would sing every Motown song we heard on the radio. We'd emulate the Temptations and Diana Ross & the Supremes. We would say that we'd love to be on Motown even though we weren't ready yet. We were just little kids singing in the bedroom, using broomsticks for microphones.

The brothers' reputation grew, and one day Katherine received a phone call from her friend Evelyn Leahy. She was organizing a children's fashion show at a department store in Forest Glen Park, about an hour away in Illinois. She wondered if the boys would sing three songs as part of the show. Katherine asked her sons and they all said yes. Evelyn needed to know the name of the group so that she could print flyers. Since the boys didn't really have a name yet, Katherine suggested the Jackson Brothers Five. Evelyn said she would shorten it—to the Jackson Five.

When the family arrived at the department store, Katherine was disappointed. There was no seating for the audience. Shoppers were going to have to stand if they wanted to hear the first-ever public show by the Jackson Five. The boys were embarrassed at first, but the enthusiastic applause at the end of their set helped them get over any misgivings.

TITO: Our very first talent show was at Theodore Roosevelt High School in Gary. That was a challenging show. One of the

groups we were competing against was called the Ethics. They were very good. They sounded just like the Temptations and could have made it big. I don't know why they didn't. We were challenged by them many times and we won at least 90 percent of the time. Another competitor of ours was Deniece Williams. She was also from Gary and she was great.

DENIECE WILLIAMS: I didn't compete in a lot of talent shows because of my involvement with the church, but when I did, I always lost to the Jackson Five. There was no hope once they hit the stage. It was over. They could sing and had stage presence. I think it was W. C. Fields who said, "Never work with children or animals." I was going up against five young children performing. It wasn't a fair fight.

At that first Roosevelt High School talent show, Jermaine sang the Temptations' hit "My Girl." Katherine put the costumes together, just as she had for the department store show and would for many years to come. Winning the talent show sent the Jackson Five into a citywide competition, where they also triumphed.

Up until this time, Joe was too busy working two shifts to give his sons much attention, let alone coach them musically. But after the talent show victories, he started them on a regular schedule of rehearsals and bought them guitars, amplifiers, and microphones.

The first paying gig for the Jackson Five was at a local club, Mister Lucky's Lounge.

JACKIE: It wasn't a very big club but it was famous in Gary. We did a really good job performing, and the people in the audience started throwing money on stage. Tito, Jermaine, and I were at the back, but Michael and Marlon were standing in the front doing some dancing, so they picked up all the money. The three of us at the back were feeling jealous because we wanted to pick up some money, too. We were so intent on watching Michael and Marlon grab all the money that we started to forget the lyrics. The next day, Michael and Marlon took their money and bought a lot of candy.

Convinced that his kids could be successful, Joe bought a VW van so he could take the

brothers and their musical instruments and equipment to Chicago to play gigs.

JACKIE: Chicago was about thirty miles from Gary. Coming from a small town, we'd go to the big city and look up at all the buildings. We were really impressed with Comiskey Park, where the Chicago White Sox played. We played in a lot of clubs in Chicago. We were too young to hang out in these clubs, so we would have to wait in a room backstage for forty minutes or so. Then we'd perform and the crowd would go crazy. After the gigs, we'd go to White Castle hamburgers on the way home. We loved those small hamburgers. We'd get home very late on a Sunday night, around two in the morning, and we'd have to take our instruments out of the car and get everything into the house. Then we'd have to wake up early and go to school.

One of the Chicago venues where Joe took his sons to play was the Regal Theater, a venue built in 1928. The theater catered to black audiences and over the years featured headliners such as Nat King Cole, B. B. King, Della Reese, and Dionne Warwick. The Jackson Five won a series of amateur nights at the Regal, which allowed them to join a bill that included some of the most popular acts of the day. One of those artists was a singer who knew what it was like to perform as a child star. Gladys Knight was only twelve years old when she started in the business. At this point in her career, she and the Pips were signed to Motown and were enjoying chart success with "I Heard It Through The Grapevine."

GLADYS KNIGHT: I was sitting in my dressing room on the second floor when I heard these little voices. I could look out from the banister to the stage, so I got up from my makeup chair and saw these little kids. I couldn't see that well because the curtains were in the way, but I could see how they moved. I thought to myself, "Oh my God, who is that?" As young as I was, I knew talent when I saw it. Even with their little children voices, I heard their potential and knew what these guys could achieve. I went back to my dressing room and when the Pips came upstairs, I asked, "Who was that singing a few minutes ago?" They told me it was "Joe's boys." I had met Joe Jackson before, just in passing. When the Pips told me who they were, I said, "We need to do something about that. I know they're here for the talent show, and if they win they'll have a leg up." The Pips said I should call Motown and get in touch with Berry Gordy. I said, "I don't think they're going to listen to us." I called the company but was told Mr. Gordy was busy. Nobody ever called back. We kept telling people about them but nobody ever came to see them. Other artists who saw the Jacksons knew what a phenomenon they were.

After the success at the Regal in Chicago, Joe loaded up the VW van for a longer trip—to New York City, where his sons would compete in the most famed amateur hour in the country, at Harlem's Apollo Theater. The Jacksons had received enough critical acclaim to be placed in the more advanced "Superdog" rounds.

JACKIE: We had never been to New York before. It was so exciting to play the Apollo, because all the major stars were there. There was a big mural on the wall with all the faces of the stars who had performed there, including James Brown, the Delfonics, Sam & Dave, Etta James, and all the Motown acts—all the musicians we idolized. That first time, we ran into Etta James. We talked to her and she was such a wonderful person, one of the nicest people we ever met. Back in those days, it was pretty rough at the Apollo if the crowd didn't like you. They would boo and throw eggs. Before we went on stage, Michael was in the wings and he saw how the crowd was treating the acts they didn't like and he was crying. He was scared because he thought they were going to do the same thing to us. I told him, "Michael, pull yourself together. Just do what you've been doing. Everything will be okay." We performed and we got a standing ovation. After, the crowd went crazy and I started crying. My eyes got so watery with joy, and I saw that Michael was happy, too. The audience in New York loved him and they loved the group.

Back home in Gary, Joe approached a local label about signing the Jackson Five. In 1968, the Steeltown imprint released "Big Boy," produced by one of the company's owners, Gordon Keith. The boys spent several consecutive Saturdays at Steeltown studios recording a number of tracks.

TITO: It felt good to have a single out. It made us feel like we were getting somewhere. We saw our record selling in stores. But we didn't realize what a small level we were at in Gary, compared to the world.

Michael wrote in *Moonwalk*, "After the records were pressed, Mr. Keith gave us some copies so we could sell them between sets and after shows. We knew that wasn't how big groups did it, but everyone had to start someplace, and in those days, having a record with your name on it was quite something."

As a hometown success story, the Jackson Five were popular enough to garner airplay for "Big Boy" on local radio station WWCA, 1270 on the AM dial. The family had advance word that the station was going to play the single for the first time, and they all gathered around the radio to hear the inaugural airplay.

Although "Big Boy" was the only single released by Steeltown before the Jacksons became famous, other tracks were recorded. Three years later, Steeltown issued the single "We Don't Have To Be Over 21 (To Fall In Love)".

"Big Boy" was enough of a regional success that Atlantic Records made a deal to distribute the single nationally through its Atco imprint. The New York-based company pressed an additional 10,000 copies, but the song's popularity didn't spread very far beyond the borders of Gary. Katherine expressed to Joe her worry that the boys were growing too old and that their chances to be signed to a national label were fading.

In July 1968, the Jackson Five was the opening act at another of Chicago's popular clubs that catered to black audiences, the High Chaparral. The headlining act was Bobby Taylor & the Vancouvers, an interracial Canadian R&B group signed to Motown. Their first single for the company, "Does Your Mama Know About Me," was cowritten by one of the Vancouvers, guitarist Tommy Chong, years before he became half of Cheech and Chong. The single was a Top 30 pop hit and a Top 5 R&B hit in the first half of 1968. Like Gladys Knight, Taylor was impressed enough with the Jackson Five to call Motown vice president Ralph Seltzer and ask him to give the boys an audition.

TOMMY CHONG: Right after the Chicago gig, Bobby invited the Jackson Five to live in his apartment in Detroit. They went directly from Chicago to Detroit. Bobby spoke to Motown and finally got them an audition. Joe [Jackson] and Bobby came to me to look at the contract, because I was the only white guy they knew. Joe handed me the contract and let me look at it. I said, "It's just for seven years. You can't go wrong in seven years."

TITO: Bobby Taylor was a young guy and he had an outgoing personality. He used to joke with us a lot. He would say, "I'm going to take your asses to Berry. He's going to hear y'all this time. Berry's got to see this." Meanwhile, we had other shows to do. We were playing the Apollo again, and we were asked to stay over in New York to do David Frost's show. That was important, because we would be seen by the whole country.

The brothers were very excited about singing on Frost's television show. So they were shocked and disappointed when their father broke the news to them that he had cancelled their appearance with Frost. Taylor had arranged the Motown audition, and it conflicted with the television appearance. Joe decided the chance to be signed to Berry Gordy's label was more important, and he loaded up the VW van and drove his sons to Detroit.

JACKIE: I remember going to Grand Boulevard. That's where the Motown studio was. And not too far down from there down the road, Berry had a house on the golf course. I remember getting out of this car and seeing him on the golf course in the distance. He called us over and said, "I'll give you $100 if you can get this ball in this hole." And $100 was a lot of money back then.

MARLON: We knew nothing about golf. He gave us a 7-iron to make the putt. You can't make a putt with a 7-iron. I know that today, but none of us did back then.

On March 11, 1969, the lives of the Jackson brothers changed forever when they signed their contract with Motown. "I was overjoyed," Katherine wrote in her autobiography *My Family, The Jacksons*. "Not only did the Motown deal mean possible stardom for the Jackson Five, but it also meant certain escape from Gary for the Jackson family."

ABOVE The Jacksons grew up in a small two-bedroom house located at 2300 Jackson Street in Gary, Indiana. They lived opposite a Little League baseball diamond. "We played a lot there," says Tito. "And foul balls from games were always landing in our yard." **OPPOSITE** The Jacksons' home was at the intersection of Jackson Street and 23rd Avenue. They only had to walk one block to Theodore Roosevelt High School, located off 24th Avenue.

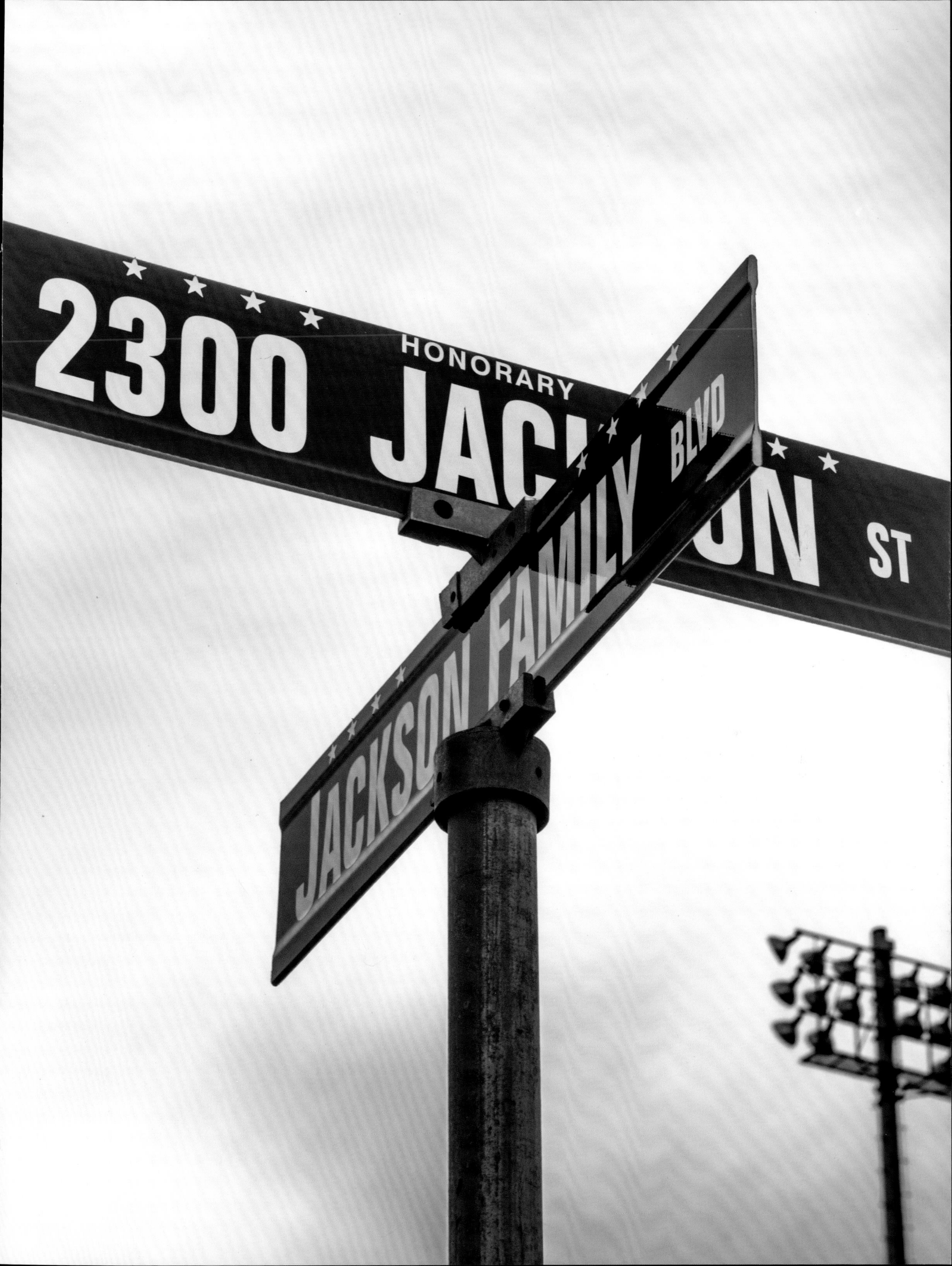
2300
HONORARY
ST
JACKSON FAMILY BLVD

JAN · 66

ABOVE The brothers recorded the very first Jackson Five single, "Big Boy," in the Steeltown studio in Gary, Indiana. **OPPOSITE** Tito still owns the guitar that his father played when he was in the Falcons. Joe warned his sons not to touch the instrument, but Tito disobeyed and one night he broke one of the strings. Joe was furious, until he heard Tito play and realized he had talent. "I still mess with it a little bit," says Tito. "There's a lot of history behind it." On the right is Jermaine's bass guitar. "I kept all the guitars, because I keep a lot of things," Tito explains. "People want to call me a hoarder, but I'm not. I have a warehouse full of things."

ABOVE Before they signed with Motown, the Jackson Five's first label was Steeltown, based in the brothers' hometown of Gary, Indiana. After an initial local release, the "Bad Boy" single was picked up for national distribution by Atlantic Records, thus the inscription: Distributed by Atco Records.
OPPOSITE These early publicity photographs of the Jackson Five were taken when they competed in various local talent contests. Their father, Joe, drove them to Chicago, where they played venues such as the Regal Theater with established acts including Bobby Taylor & the Vancouvers.

Source: Chicago Daily Defender, Aug. 11, 1968

THE MOTOWN YEARS.

THE JACKSON 5 RELOCATE TO DETROIT AND MOVE IN WITH BOBBY TAYLOR, WHO PRODUCES A NUMBER OF TRACKS FOR THEM. MOTOWN THEN MOVES THE FAMILY TO LOS ANGELES, WHERE THEY LIVE WITH DIANA ROSS AND WORK WITH PRODUCERS KNOWN AS THE CORPORATION. THE FIRST SINGLE, "I WANT YOU BACK," TOPS THE CHART, AS DO THE NEXT THREE SINGLES. WITHIN A FEW MONTHS, THE JACKSON BROTHERS ARE FAMOUS ALL OVER THE WORLD.

AFTER WRITING AND producing songs for other record labels, Berry Gordy took the advice of his friend Smokey Robinson and, with an $800 loan from his family, created the Motown Record Corporation. He wanted to name his first label "Tammy," after the Debbie Reynolds movie, but for legal reasons went with "Tamla." Motown established its own publishing arm, Jobete, and a talent agency to manage its artists.

The first successful single was "Shop Around," a No. 2 hit for the Miracles that debuted on the *Billboard* Hot 100 the week of December 12, 1960. The 1960s proved to be a golden decade for Motown, with twenty No. 1 singles in the USA from an array of artists that included the Marvelettes, Stevie Wonder, Mary Wells, the Supremes, the Four Tops, the Temptations, and Marvin Gaye.

At the beginning of the 1970s, Motown took a couple of sharp turns. Its biggest act, Diana Ross & the Supremes, divided in two. Ross performed with Mary Wilson and Cindy Birdsong for the last time on January 14, 1970, before launching her solo career. The Supremes continued as a trio with a new lead singer, Jean Terrell. At the same time, the label's newest act was hurtling toward the top of the chart. With their name now presented as the Jackson 5, instead of the spelled-out Jackson Five, the group achieved pole position the week of January 31, 1970, with their single "I Want You Back."

Motown spent the better part of 1969 grooming the five brothers from Gary, Indiana, for stardom. First, they traveled to Detroit and went into the studio with Bobby Taylor, the Motown artist who had brought them to the attention of the company. They weren't only working with Taylor; they moved into his apartment, too.

MARLON JACKSON: We stayed with Bobby and his wife in their apartment in Detroit. She taught us how to swim. We used to rehearse and go to the studio to work with Bobby on the first album. Bobby was a jokester, but he knew what he wanted in the studio. He was a lot of help to us because he was a great singer.

JACKIE JACKSON: We slept on cots and on the floor. He had this big apartment and we were always learning new songs before going to the studio.

After the Jacksons signed their contract with Motown, one of Berry's first requests

of the group was to sing at Diana Ross's birthday party in March 1969.

TITO JACKSON: It was the first time we met any of the Motown stars. We were in heaven, because so many of the people we admired were there. Some of the Temptations were there, and Marvin Gaye and Tammi Terrell, Martha Reeves, some of the Four Tops. Motown was a very close-knit company. The stars knew each other and hung out together. It was run more like a family company than a corporation.

In his biography *Moonwalk*, Michael recalled meeting another Motown star. "I remember when I first shook Smokey Robinson's hand. It was like shaking hands with a king. My eyes lit up with stars, and I remember telling my mother that his hand felt as if it was layered with soft pillows…. When I think about it now, it sounds silly, but it made a big impression on me."

TITO: The Motown staff were very kind to us. They treated us like children. Everybody was like our father and mother. They were just very nice to us. So we did our performance at the party, around the indoor pool. We sang our own songs to them and watched their reactions. They all seemed to really like us. I remember going back to Gary, bragging that we were signed to Motown. Our friends were very supportive, and we told them we were going back to Detroit in two weeks to start a record, which is what happened.

JACKIE: Our band was set up around the pool. It was two hours before show time and my brothers were running around playing. Berry Gordy had a bowling alley. He had a big arcade room and they had never seen anything like it. We were kids from Gary, Indiana, who had never been in a big mansion. I looked at my watch and was nervous, and I noticed Smokey Robinson and Stevie Wonder. We had to sing their own songs in front of them. My brothers were running around, having fun and playing like little kids. They forgot that we had a show to do and that it was make it or break it for us. I was yelling at them, and they just said, "Come on Jackie, it's going to be okay." I told them, "No man, you don't understand. They're here and we're singing their songs." I was trying to let them know what was going on. They didn't quite get it. Then when we performed, all of the Motown artists

clapped. It felt good to be singing their songs, and afterwards they all came over and hugged us.

Some of the Motown stars, such as Mary Wilson from the Supremes, already knew about the Jackson 5.

MARY WILSON: We had worked with Bobby Taylor & the Vancouvers in Canada and became close with them. Bobby told us about the Jacksons and said they were fabulous and we had to see them. Once we did, we realized they were not only great, they were perfection. It was very obvious they had been brought up on music, especially artists like Jackie Wilson. We knew someone had given them that kind of direction, and it was their dad. When we saw them, they were already polished. They didn't need to go through Motown's artist development.

Jackie and his brothers had no idea how well they would get to know the Motown artists. When the label's headquarters relocated from Detroit to Los Angeles, Gordy decided to move the Jacksons to Southern California. Joe quit his job at Inland Steel and headed for Los Angeles in the family's new Dodge Maxivan, with Tito, drummer Johnny Jackson (no relation), and keyboard player Ronnie Rancifer. Katherine stayed in Gary with LaToya, Randy, and Janet. Jackie, Jermaine, Marlon, and Michael boarded a flight to the Golden State.

JACKIE: We had been driving in the family VW van to all of our gigs in other cities, so we had never flown on a jet before. Getting on a plane and flying west was really special. My ears were popping, exploding like crazy. And once we landed, my eyes were burning because there was so much smog. The air was pure and fresh in Gary. But it was incredible seeing the palm trees in LA and all the fancy cars driving down the street. We felt like we were in paradise.

MARLON: When we first came to Los Angeles, we stayed in a motel on Santa Monica Boulevard for a month. It was called the Tropicana and it was owned by Sandy Koufax, the pitcher for the Dodgers.

JACKIE: Berry invited us to live with him, and after that we moved into Diana Ross's house. She was incredible. She took us under her wing and taught us all about the music business; Berry Gordy did the same thing. They prepped us about what it was going to be like, doing interviews and things like that.

MARLON: Everything was white at Diana's house. I mean, white carpet, white chairs, white everything. We did a lot of painting, and she would paint with us. We got paint all over everything but she didn't seem to mind. Later, when she moved to Beverly Hills, Michael and I came over and spent the whole day. Diana was pregnant with her daughter Rhonda. Michael, Diana, and I painted designs on the drapes that she was going to hang up in her baby's room.

TITO: Diana was very motherly. She looked after us like her own children. Her home was in the Hollywood Hills, just down the street from where Berry lived. We used to go to his place all the time to swim and play basketball and games. He'd pull out the boxing gloves. Motown was a fun company to be with. But we were only children and we didn't realize what a golden time it was. It was so nice to be in Diana's home in Hollywood, looking at the lights of the city below. You can imagine how we felt, coming from Gary, Indiana—we were blown away. Everyone was so good to us. They made sure we got our meals, had breakfast and dinner, and they let us go to the park and made sure we had a little change in our pockets. There was always somebody watching over us, an adult to make sure everything was cool. They took excellent care of us.

When it was time to show off the Jackson 5 to the world for the first time, Motown chose an exclusive private club in Beverly Hills.

MARY WILSON: I remember getting an invitation to The Daisy. It was where Motown was going to introduce the group to the public.

The Daisy was located on chic Rodeo Drive. It was a hang-out for stars such as Robert Redford, Natalie Wood, Barbra Streisand, Warren Beatty, Jack Nicholson, and Fred Astaire. Items on the menu were named after the members of the club—for example, the Jack Lemmon fresh fruit and cottage cheese bowl or the Katharine Hepburn hamburger. On August 11, 1969, some 350 guests showed up to see Diana Ross introduce the five youngsters from Gary. Those guests were told a slightly

different version of the truth: that Diana had discovered the Jackson 5, and that lead singer Michael was eight years old (he was a few days shy of his eleventh birthday). But it made for good press.

JACKIE: We were really nervous about performing at The Daisy because we were in Beverly Hills and Berry Gordy had invited all of these celebrities and movie stars that he knew, as well as other singers. We met Fred Williamson. Bill Cosby was there and Robert Culp was with him. Hugh Hefner was there, too— they were all friends with Berry. There are a lot of things you have to do if you want to make it. You have to do those kind of shows so people can see you perform. We didn't sing any originals because we didn't have any. So we sang Motown hits. It was a great show and the guests loved it; we did well. Personally, I thought we did horribly, but I'm always thinking that. I'm never satisfied; I'm always hard on myself. But the people loved it, and that's all that mattered.

Five days after being introduced to the world at The Daisy, the Jackson 5 played their first show for the public as a Motown act.

JACKIE: The first thing we knew about it was when my father told us, "You guys are going to do a concert. You've got to do at least an hour-and-a-half show." We didn't have enough songs to fill ninety minutes. Then we found out we only needed to be on stage for less than twenty minutes— but we would be in front of 18,000 people! It was amazing and scary.

The Jackson 5 were unannounced special guests at a Diana Ross & the Supremes concert at the Forum in Inglewood, California. In the middle of the Supremes' set, Diana surprised the audience by bringing out Motown's newest act.

JACKIE: Backstage, we were really nervous, but that went away once we began performing. We didn't see Diana before we went out because she was too busy preparing for her live show. We did get to watch the Supremes perform from our place backstage, and then we had to get into our lime green outfits—which our mother had made for us—and get ready to be introduced.

TITO: There was a stage that revolved and we came out and did our little thing

for about fifteen minutes. It was before "I Want You Back" was released. I remember one of the songs we did was "Stand!" by Sly & the Family Stone.

MARLON: [Motown executive] Suzanne de Passe was in charge of us, and when it was time to go on stage, she told us, "Go out there and do your thing." I can understand why Berry put her with us. She had enough sense to keep us in line, but she was only twenty-three, not much older than us. We worked really hard, but we would go ice skating or bowling, too. When we were on tour, we would take a week off and go to Lake Geneva and go horseback riding because that would release the stress. We would wrestle and have pillow fights. We had a lot of fun together.

For those not lucky enough to be at The Daisy or the Forum to see the Jackson 5, there was television. The quintet made two important network appearances in the fall of 1969. On October 18, the brothers were guests on ABC-TV'S *The Hollywood Palace*. Diana Ross was the host for that episode, and the boys introduced "I Want You Back" to America. Then, on December 14, the Jackson 5 made their first appearance on *The Ed Sullivan Show*.

JACKIE: We always wanted to be on Ed Sullivan. When we were in Gary, we watched his show every Sunday night. That's where we would see Sam Cooke, the Everly Brothers, and Johnny Mathis. Being on the show was a dream come true for us. It was exciting to meet Ed Sullivan. He was a nice guy, a real nice fellow. And in person, he was exactly the same as you saw him on the show.

Hollywood wasn't only about performing on stage and having fun. The five brothers also spent a lot of time in the recording studio. After working with Bobby Taylor in Detroit, Berry Gordy introduced the Jacksons to a new production team in Los Angeles: Deke Richards, Freddie Perren, and Fonce Mizell, who were known collectively as the Corporation.

TITO: Those guys were geniuses. They had all studied music in college. They had us record a song a day. Right after school, we'd go to the studio and knock out a song. We could do an album in a week or two. Deke was very mellow and serious about his music. They all treated us very well.

The Corporation had been working on a song for Gladys Knight, "I Wanna Be Free." But when they brought it to Berry Gordy for his approval, the Motown founder suggested some rewrites and told the three writer-producers that the song would be better for a new group he had just signed. "I Wanna Be Free" became "I Want You Back."

JACKIE: I remember going into the Motown studio and hearing the track coming through big studio monitors right in our face. It was slamming. The intro was so strong. Berry always taught us to have a strong intro to get people's attention right away. And I remember the Corporation teaching us the song. Michael picked it up so fast; it was easy to learn for all of us. They kept changing it here and there for the better. We told them it was great, but the next day Freddie and Fonce added more things to it. They wanted to make it perfect. Michael did these ad-libs at the end of the song. They didn't teach him that; he just made up his own stuff. They let him do his thing and he used to come up with incredible stuff.

Before the Jackson 5 recorded "I Want You Back," Perren wondered if their lead singer could hit the high E-flat note that was required. "I worried about that more than anything else," Perren told Adam White in *The Billboard Book of Number One Rhythm & Blues Hits.* "Michael wasn't as outgoing or playful as the other guys. He would just stand there...and all the time I was showing it to him, I was thinking, 'Can he reach these notes?' Finally, we took a try at it and he hit it the first time." When the track was ready, Perren, Mizell, and Richards took it to Berry Gordy for his seal of approval. "He said, 'Oh man, you guys are getting ready to blow a hit,'" Perren told White. "'Get the fellas back and do some more rehearsing.' So we shaped them up and worked a couple more days."

JACKIE: When I heard "I Want You Back" on the radio for the first time, I was driving in my car by myself on Fairfax in LA and I pulled over to the side of the road. Hearing your song for the first time on the radio is unbelievable. You hear it in the studio all the time, but when you hear it on the radio, it sounds ten times better. And I remember we recorded it just off Fairfax. We would get out of school and the studio was right there, not even a hundred yards away. The kids at Fairfax High School had no idea we were recording songs in the studio around the corner.

"I Want You Back" debuted on the *Billboard* Hot 100 the week of November 15, 1969. Eleven weeks later, the song was No. 1.

JACKIE: I was at home and got a call from Suzanne de Passe to let us know we were No. 1. I didn't want to wait for them to send us a copy of *Billboard*, so I went right out and bought five copies. There we were, on top of the pop and R&B charts, in front of all the other acts. There's nothing more exciting than to be No. 1 with your very first record. We worked so hard in the recording studio, and it paid off.

The same team that wrote and produced "I Want You Back" put together the follow-up. "On the chorus part to 'I Want You Back,' it comes around to the end and Michael sings, 'I want you back, yeah, yeah, yeah.' The music of 'ABC' is right there," Perren told Adam White in *The Billboard Book of Number One Rhythm & Blues Hits.* "We just took that music and kept playing it. However, it wasn't that simple—it had to be fashioned into a real song. It was thought out, we didn't just get around and start singing little catchy phrases and rhymes. It was thought out to coincide with the fact that [the Jackson 5] were the age they were, and most of their fans were in school."

JACKIE: At first, I didn't like "ABC." I thought it was too "kiddieland," but when the Corporation brought in the first guitar, they got my attention. That's when I thought, "Oh, wait a minute. You might have a great song here." Even today, my three-year-old twins love it and walk around the house singing it. I think "ABC" will always be around because all the little kids love that song. It's true, after "I Want You Back," they went back to the same drawing board to make a perfect song. Being in the recording studio with Deke Richards was like going to college at Motown. Berry would come in and change something in the studio. We'd watch everything he was doing because that's how we learned.

TITO: The Corporation was unique, because they would add elements to the track like foot stomps and handclaps, but in a whole different way from anyone else. They were just more modern with everything. I think that's what made us stand out at the time.

The Jackson 5 introduced "ABC" to the nation on *American Bandstand.* First,

the youngsters sang "I Want You Back," then they were interviewed by Dick Clark. There was only one problem. Dick asked Michael to introduce the individual members of the group and the pre-teen star-in-the-making instinctively took the mic from the host. Dick was accustomed to holding his own mic and extending it to the guest artist when he asked his questions. He took it back and told Michael, "I feel very naked without a microphone. I've been holding one of these things...a long time." When Dick asked his next question, somehow the mic ended up back in Michael's hands. Exasperated and uncomfortable, Dick said, on air, "Hey Mike, can I have the mic back? Just for a second!" They both laughed, and Michael smiled as he handed the mic back to Clark. It was a great moment of television and also marked the beginning of years of friendship between Clark and the Jackson family. The issue resolved, and the mic firmly back in Clark's hands, the *Bandstand* host then said, "I think this is the first time this record has been played on the air and it's about to be released. It's a thing called 'ABC'?" he asked Michael, who affirmed the title before heading off to perform the group's second Motown single.

"ABC" debuted on the *Billboard* Hot 100 the week of March 14, 1970, and six weeks later it repeated the success of "I Want You Back" by climbing into pole position. It didn't take very long for Motown to issue a third single by the Jackson 5. "The Love You Save" was also written and produced by the Corporation.

JACKIE: We did a lot of work on "The Love You Save." Berry Gordy came into the studio so many times to get it right. The Corporation had all the ingredients, but they were trying to put the ingredients together to make the song a hit. They had changed things around on the first two songs, but on this one they were seriously moving things around. It was like playing chess. In the end, they really got it together.

Perren told Adam White in *The Billboard Book of Number One Rhythm & Blues Hits,* "We kept a lot of the ingredients in there. There was a little play between Jermaine and Michael; we always tried to get that in there. We found out Tito had a commercial bass voice and we would put little trick things in with him." The Corporation produced their demo version of "The Love You Save" one night. "I didn't realize how raggedy it was," Perren said. "But it said what it was supposed to say, so that when some real pros got on it, they could play it right."

"The Love You Save" entered the *Billboard* Hot 100 the week of May 30, 1970, and was No. 1 a mere four weeks later.

JACKIE: With the third No. 1, people started noticing where we were going. Our lives began to change. Everywhere we went, there were girls screaming, even in our classroom at Fairfax High. We were still going to school then, and a lot of kids in the class didn't know who I was. Girls would come to the classroom door, just screaming. They were coming from other schools, too. People would look around and ask, "Who are they screaming for?" I knew who they were screaming for, but no one else knew. I was very quiet in school.

Three No. 1s—not bad. But that wasn't the end of the run. The fourth Jackson 5 single on Motown was scheduled to be another Corporation production, "Mama's Pearl." Years before Berry Gordy moved Motown from Detroit to Hollywood, he opened up a West Coast office and asked producer Hal Davis to be in charge. In that capacity, he was the person from Motown who picked up the Jacksons at the airport when they arrived in California. Soon after, Davis received a song written by a friend of his, Bob West. Motown's A&R department didn't give the tune much consideration, and they certainly weren't thinking of the Jackson 5 when they heard it, as the group was in a hit-making groove with the Corporation.

HAL DAVIS: Very few tunes have come along in my lifetime that I knew were just natural. This particular tune was natural. I first heard it on just the keyboards. I loved the melody—the title was already "I'll Be There" but I thought it needed some help with the lyrics.

Davis and West rewrote the song with Motown artist Willie Hutch. "Mr. Gordy liked the title and the track but he didn't like the song," Hutch told Adam White in *The Billboard Book of Number One Rhythm & Blues Hits*. "Hal came to my house at about 3:45 in the morning. He felt I could get the song done." Sure enough, ninety minutes later Hutch had revised the composition. He came up with two ways to go: "One was more or less a brotherhood kind of lyric, and the other was more guy-girl." By eight o'clock in the morning, Hutch and Davis were at Gordy's mansion. "Berry listened for

about fifteen minutes and said, 'OK, that's a smash. Set up studio time for one o'clock.'"

TITO: We didn't know it was going to be a single. We just recorded the songs the company gave us. We would finish an album, and the company would issue the songs that it felt strongly about. But I think it was a good move to release "I'll Be There" because it showed the group was versatile, that we weren't just about up-tempo, young songs. The lyrics were adult but sounded great for the young voice of Michael, with the rest of us doing the background vocals.

"I'll Be There" debuted on the *Billboard* Hot 100 the week of September 19, 1970, and reached the top four weeks later. The single stayed at No. 1 for five weeks, becoming not only the biggest hit for the Jackson 5, but also the best-selling Motown 45 to date, surpassing Marvin Gaye's 1968 chart-topper "I Heard It Through The Grapevine." The Jackson 5 made chart history by becoming the first—and so far only—group to have its first four singles all reach No. 1.

Motown followed the adult ballad with the Corporation's "Mama's Pearl," which broke the string of No. 1s by peaking at No. 2. For the sixth Jackson 5 single, the company turned again to producer Hal Davis for "Never Can Say Goodbye," a tune written by Broadway actor Clifton Davis. Through singer/songwriter Gloria Jones, who had cowritten "If I Were Your Woman" for Gladys Knight & the Pips, Clifton was introduced to executives at Motown.

CLIFTON DAVIS: I had a song I had written for the Supremes called "Here Comes The Sunrise." I got them together backstage in Las Vegas and played them the song on piano. They said, "If you can stick around until tomorrow, our producer will be coming to town and you can play it for him." So I stayed and played it for Frank Wilson and he loved it. A couple of weeks later, I got a call from Jobete Music. Could I come to California and sign a publishing contract? So I jumped on a plane, went to Jobete, and in walked Hal Davis. I told him I had a song for the Jackson 5. I had written it a year-and-a-half earlier. I played it for him and he said, "Clifton, that's a smash."

Davis was inspired to write "Never Can Say Goodbye" by his childhood, when his parents separated and he lived part-time

with each one. Every time he had to leave his mother or his father, he was so upset that he would cry. So he literally never could say goodbye.

CLIFTON DAVIS: The Jackson 5 recorded the song, and then Berry Gordy asked me to do a melody rewrite on a little portion of it. So I rewrote the melody with Michael there, so he could learn the new part. They went back into the studio right away. Michael was young, but he was professional. His ear and pitch were amazing. He could take things and make them his own.

"Never Can Say Goodbye" also peaked at No. 2. It was covered so quickly by Isaac Hayes that his version was on the Hot 100 simultaneously with the Jackson 5 original. Hayes's single peaked at No. 22. Three-and-a-half years later, Gloria Gaynor recorded a disco version. Her single went to No. 9.

GLORIA GAYNOR: I loved the song so much that I did it in every show, but when it was time to record it myself, I struggled to do a unique version and not to sing it like Michael. The producer sent me home with the track to practice and to come up with a different way of singing it. I was hopeful it would be a hit for me, but the positive response to my version of the song was definitely greater than I expected, and a wonderful surprise. Since then, I've been on the same show with the Jackson 5 a couple of times, but I've never talked to them about the song or had an on-stage performance with them.

The Jackson 5 weren't only having success on the singles charts. Their first album, *Diana Ross Presents The Jackson 5*, with a title meant to give credence to the myth that Ross discovered the Jacksons, peaked at No. 5. Less than six months later, a second album was released. *ABC* reached No. 4. Two more LPs were released in 1970: *Third Album* also went to No. 4, while the *Jackson 5 Christmas Album* didn't chart—not unusual at the time for holiday-themed sets.

The Jackson 5 was easily Motown's most successful act in the first half of the 1970s. They toured the UK, Africa, and Australia, they starred on television specials, they were featured on a Saturday morning animated television series, and they had millions of fans all over the world. It seemed like the Jackson 5's run at Motown would never end—but all good things…

MARLON JACKSON:

"MY FATHER RULED WITH AN IRON FIST. SOMETIMES HE WOULD COME HOME AT THREE IN THE MORNING AND HE'D WAKE US UP AND HAVE US DO A CHORE OVER AGAIN. THE LESSON WAS, WE NEEDED TO GET IT RIGHT THE FIRST TIME."

OPPOSITE These stills are from the audition tape that was sent to Berry Gordy so he could decide if he wanted to sign the Jackson 5 to the Motown label.

OPPOSITE AND ABOVE The brothers were photographed in various locations in Detroit, wearing identical outfits made for them by a tailor in Chicago. **OVERLEAF** In 1969, photographer Lawrence Schiller shot a series of photographs on the beach in Malibu, California, with [L to R] Tito, Marlon, Jackie, Jermaine, and Michael.

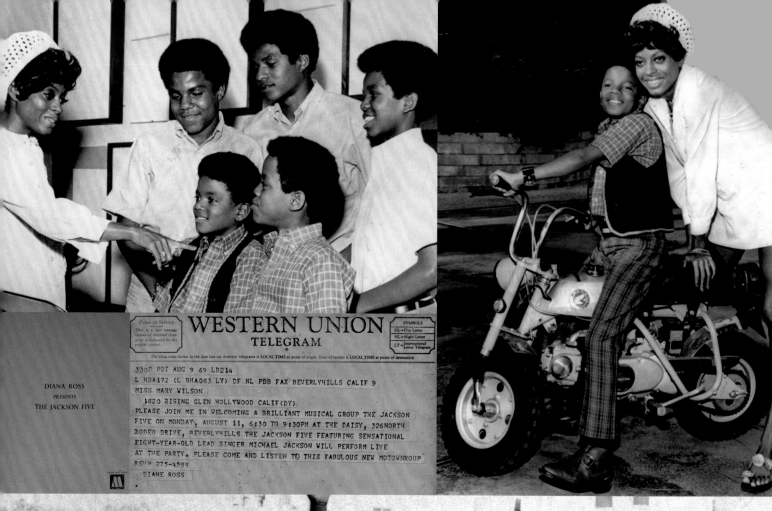

WESTERN UNION
TELEGRAM

CLASS OF SERVICE
This is a fast message unless its deferred character is indicated by the proper symbol.

SYMBOLS
DL = Day Letter
NL = Night Letter
LT = International Letter Telegram

The filing time shown in the date line on domestic telegrams is LOCAL TIME at point of origin. Time of receipt is LOCAL TIME at point of destination

330P PDT AUG 9 69 LD214

L HDA172 (L BHA083 LY) DF NL PDB FAX BEVERLYHILLS CALIF 9
MISS MARY WILSON

1820 RISING GLEN HOLLYWOOD CALIF(DY)
PLEASE JOIN ME IN WELCOMING A BRILLIANT MUSICAL GROUP THE JACKSON
FIVE ON MONDAY, AUGUST 11, 6:30 TO 9:30PM AT THE DAISY, 326NORTH
RODEO DRIVE, BEVERLYHILLS THE JACKSON FIVE FEATURING SENSATIONAL
EIGHT-YEAR-OLD LEAD SINGER MICHAEL JACKSON WILL PERFORM LIVE
AT THE PARTY. PLEASE COME AND LISTEN TO THIS FABULOUS NEW MOTOWNROUP
RSVP 275-4588

DIANE ROSS

JACKIE JACKSON:

"WE HAD A GREAT TIME LIVING IN DIANA ROSS'S HOME. SHE HAD A CHEF COOKING ALL OF OUR MEALS. WE HAD NEVER EXPERIENCED ANYTHING LIKE THAT BEFORE. WE PLAYED A LOT, BUT WHENEVER IT WAS TIME TO WORK, WE WENT TO WORK."

OPPOSITE Publicity photographs of the brothers with Motown's top star, Diana Ross, helped to perpetrate the myth that the lead singer of the Supremes discovered the Jackson 5. In fact, Gladys Knight and Bobby Taylor were the first Motown artists to bring the youngsters from Gary, Indiana, to the attention of the record label. Telegrams sent as invitations, including this one that was delivered to Mary Wilson of the Supremes, also made it seem as if Diana was responsible for bringing the quintet to Berry Gordy.

ABOVE The Jackson 5's first Motown single was "I Want You Back," which entered the US singles chart on November 15, 1969. The flip side was a song the group had been performing before they signed with Berry Gordy's label: a cover of the Miracles' "Who's Lovin' You." Years later, the Smokey Robinson composition became a popular audition song on *American Idol*, although the young contestants only knew the Jackson 5 version. **OPPOSITE** "I Want You Back" was issued as a single all over the world, and every country had its own artwork.

Portugal

Germany

Israel

Japan

Netherlands

Italy

Yugoslavia

Spain

Sweden

Norway

France

Turkey

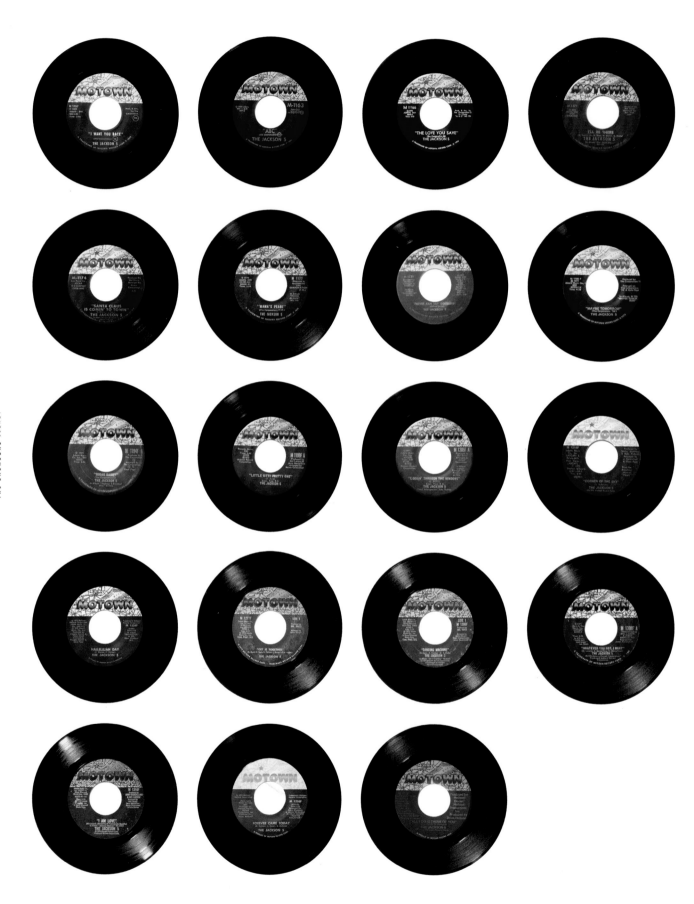

OPPOSITE This collection comprises all of the Jackson 5's Motown singles, from "I Want You Back" in 1969 to "All I Do Is Think Of You" in 1975. **ABOVE** These images are from one of the earliest photo sessions for the Jackson 5 after they signed with Motown. They soon became one of the most photographed groups in the label's history.

OPPOSITE Taken during the same session that produced the cover image for the Jackson 5's first Motown album, any one of these shots could have adorned the front of the LP. **ABOVE** When the Jackson 5 started work on their first Motown album, their initial producer was Bobby Taylor, who was at the helm for tracks such as covers of Marvin Gaye's "Chained," Stevie Wonder's "My Cherie Amour," and Sly & the Family Stone's "Stand!" Then Berry Gordy brought in the Corporation, who wrote and produced the group's first single, "I Want You Back." **OVERLEAF** On December 14, 1969, millions of Americans were introduced to the Jackson 5 when they made their first appearance on *The Ed Sullivan Show*. Marlon recalls, "Suzanne de Passe and her cousin Tony Jones took Michael and I to Fred Segal's clothing store on Melrose in Los Angeles to buy our outfits for our appearance on *Ed Sullivan* because they couldn't find anything else to fit us."

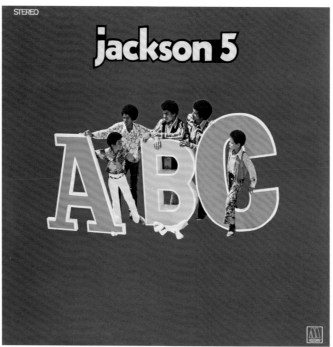

ABOVE When Motown released the second Jackson 5 album, the title song had already been a No. 1 hit on the *Billboard* Hot 100. After the LP came out, Motown issued another track as the follow-up to "ABC." "The Love You Save" also soared to No. 1.

ABOVE For musicians who wanted to play "I Want You Back" and "ABC" with their own bands, Motown's publishing arm released the sheet music to those two singles and other Jackson 5 tracks.

MARLON JACKSON:

"WE MADE MUSIC BECAUSE WE ENJOYED DOING IT. WE WERE HAVING FUN, NOT REALIZING WHAT WAS GOING TO COME AFTER THAT. BUT IT HAPPENED. ALSO, IT WAS ONE OF THE BEST ERAS FOR MUSIC, AND NOT BECAUSE WE WERE PART OF IT."

OPPOSITE Michael Jackson was thirteen years old when this photograph was taken at the family home in Encino, California, in early 1972. Even when he was young, Michael was always more comfortable with a microphone in his hand. When the Jackson 5 made their first appearance on *American Bandstand* in 1970, Michael repeatedly took the mic from host Dick Clark, even after Clark joked with him and asked him not to.

ABOVE The Jackson 5 had been popular for more than six months when they appeared on an August cover of *Jet* magazine. Unfortunately, the editors misidentified Jackie as Jermaine and Jermaine as "Sigmund," Jackie's legal name. **OPPOSITE** The brothers had fun play fighting at this photo session: (L to R) Tito, Jackie, Michael, Marlon, and Jermaine.

OPPOSITE He ain't heavy; he's my brother: Michael and Marlon sit on the shoulders of their older brothers Jermaine, Jackie, and Tito. **ABOVE** Released on September 8, 1970, the Jackson 5's third album was titled *Third Album* and contained three singles: "I'll Be There," "Mama's Pearl," and "Goin' Back To Indiana."

ABOVE Although their Christmas album has become a seasonal favorite, the Jacksons didn't enjoy making the record. "We had just finished working on the *Third Album* and it took forever. We had one day off and then we started working on the Christmas album." Jackie explains, "It was hard work and I wanted to enjoy the summer a little bit. It was 95 degrees outside and we were singing about Christmas. But the album turned out really well and is one of my favorites." **OPPOSITE** The Jackson brothers wore a lot of fringe in the 1970s, as seen here on Tito and Michael in the group's holiday publicity photograph.

SOUL
America's Most Soulful Newspaper

JUNE 1, 1970 · 25¢

The **Jackson 5** *World's Most Soulful Family*

SPECIAL: FOURTH ANNIVERSARY / ARETHA GETS $5-MILLION

SOUL
June 15, 1970 · 25¢

A CLOSE-UP of JACKIE of The Jackson 5

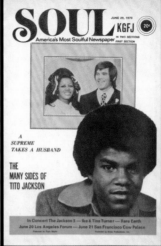

SOUL
America's Most Soulful Newspaper

KGFJ · JUNE 29, 1970 · 20¢

A SUPREME TAKES A HUSBAND

THE MANY SIDES OF TITO JACKSON

In Concert The Jackson 5 — Ike & Tina Turner — Rare Earth
June 20 Los Angeles Forum · June 21 San Francisco Cow Palace

EARL GRANT DEAD AT 39

SOUL
America's Most Soulful Newspaper

KGFJ · JULY 13, 1970 · 20¢

JERMAINE JACKSON RAPS ON GIRLS

ARETHA RETURNS

In Concert The Jackson 5 — Ike & Tina Turner — Rare Earth
June 20 Los Angeles Forum — June 19 San Francisco Cow Palace

LIVE PERFORMANCE PICS OF J-5

SOUL
America's Most Soulful Newspaper

July 27, 1970 · 25¢

Marlon Jackson: the loveable one

ARETHA WOMAN of the YEAR

SOUL
America's Most Soulful Newspaper

IN TWO SECTIONS FIRST SECTION · 20¢

MICHAEL . . .

SOUL
America's Most Soulful Newspaper

KGFJ · March 22, 1971 · 25¢

Jackson Five vs. Osmond Brothers

SOUL WAR COMING?

SOUL
America's Most Soulful Newspaper

KGFJ · March 6, 1972 · 25¢

SMOKEY ROBINSON QUITS

JACKIE TO LEAVE HOME AFTER CLOSE BRUSH

Gladys and the Pips at Demo Convention

SOUL
America's Most Soulful Newspaper

August 28, 1972 · 15¢

What Kind of Girl Did Tito Jackson Marry?

SOUL
America's Most Soulful Newspaper

September 11, 1972 · 35¢ · KDIA

Jermaine Jackson Tells All . . .

NATIONAL Edition

SOUL
America's Most Soulful Newspaper

35¢ · June 25, 1973

JACKSON 5 Work is fun in Japan!

Jackson family arrives in Japan

NATIONAL Edition

SOUL
America's Most Soulful Newspaper

25¢ · July 23, 1973

Tito & Jermaine: What Turns Them On?

• Sly's gonna be a daddy!
• Aretha shines
• Ronny Dyson
• Cinema, Jazz & More

MICHAEL JACKSON IN *MOONWALK*:

"I REMEMBER BERRY GORDY... SAYING THAT WE WERE GOING TO MAKE HISTORY TOGETHER. 'I'M GONNA MAKE YOU THE BIGGEST THING IN THE WORLD,' HE SAID, 'AND YOU'RE GONNA BE WRITTEN ABOUT IN HISTORY BOOKS.'"

PREVIOUS "I always enjoyed the feeling of being on stage," Michael told *Interview* magazine in 1982. "When I hit the stage it's like all of a sudden a magic from somewhere just comes, and the spirit just hits you and you lose control of yourself." **OPPOSITE** Husband and wife Ken and Regina Jones launched the weekly newspaper *Soul* in 1966. The publication focused on black entertainers and featured the Jackson 5 on its cover many times—as a group and as individuals.

ABOVE Michael, Jackie, and Tito graced the front cover of the Jackson 5's fifth album, *Maybe Tomorrow*, while Marlon and Jermaine appeared on the back cover. Released in 1971, it was the first Jackson 5 LP to miss the Top 5, peaking at No. 11 on *Billboard*'s album chart. There were only two singles released from *Maybe Tomorrow*: "Never Can Say Goodbye" and the title track. **OPPOSITE** This family portrait was taken at the Jacksons' home in Encino, California, with (L to R) Michael, Marlon, Tito, Jermaine, Jackie, Joe, and Katherine surrounded by framed charts from *Billboard* and *Cash Box*, and gold and platinum awards for millions of records shipped to stores.

PREVIOUS The family gathered in the backyard of their Encino home to admire the brothers' brand new motorcycles, purchased from a store on Santa Monica Boulevard. Did their parents approve of them riding the bikes? "They drove us to the store to buy them," says Jackie. "But they made us wear helmets when we were riding."

OPPOSITE AND ABOVE "Being in the Jackson 5 was a full-time job," says Jackie. "We stayed busy all the time. If we weren't recording, we were doing photo sessions—more photo sessions than we could count, wearing all kinds of outfits."

CHAPTER TWO · THE MOTOWN YEARS

OPPOSITE ABOVE In their television special *Goin' Back To Indiana*, which aired on ABC on September 19, 1971, the Jacksons were called on to act in an eight-minute comedy sketch titled "The Day Basketball Was Saved." **OPPOSITE BELOW** The Jackson 5 performed "I Want You Back" on *Goin' Back To Indiana*. **ABOVE** The sixth album released by the Jackson 5 was the soundtrack to *Goin' Back To Indiana*. It was issued by Motown ten days after the television program aired.

THE ANDY WILLIAMS SHOW 1-31-70 The Jackson 5 tried out some new choreography when they performed "I Want You Back" on the eighteenth episode of the first season of NBC-TV's *The Andy Williams Show*.

THE CAROL BURNETT SHOW 3-16-74 "Carol was very nice," says Marlon. "We really enjoyed doing her show. In one of the skits, her writers came up with nicknames for each of us. She called me 'the dancingest Jackson.'"

THE MIKE DOUGLAS SHOW 4-3-74 Douglas and co-host Dom DeLuise interviewed the Jackson 5 and quickly noticed there were six of them. Youngest brother Randy performed with the group as they sang their new single "Dancing Machine."

THE MIDNIGHT SPECIAL 2-2-79 The Jacksons performed "Shake Your Body (Down To The Ground)" on NBC-TV's late-night music series, broadcast every Friday.

ABOVE In the cover story of the September 1970 issue of *Ebony*, reporter Louie Robinson predicted that the youngest Jackson brother, Randy (aged eight at the time), would one day join the Jackson 5. A year later, the Jackson 5 were again featured on the cover of *Ebony*. This time the accompanying article focused on the Saturday morning *Jackson 5ive* series and the ABC television special *Goin' Back To Indiana*.
OPPOSITE The source of the September 1971 cover of *Ebony* was this advertisement for ABC's animated series *Jackson 5ive*, which premiered on September 11, 1971.

Published by
Raydell Publishing &
Distributing Corp.
311 West 43rd Street
New York, N. Y. 10036

For additional
copies mail $2.25

Jackson
5ive

See the Jackson Five animated series
on ABC-TV Network every Saturday
morning. Produced in Association with
Rankin / Bass.

THE MOTOWN SOUND

ABOVE *The Jackson 5 TV Book* was published in 1971 and included twenty-four pages of photographs. There were illustrations from the animated series and color photographs of each member of the group, accompanied by biographies. The book also contained sheet music to the songs featured on the *Jackson 5ive* series. **OPPOSITE** Arthur Rankin, Jr. and Jules Bass owned the company that produced *Jackson 5ive*, which aired on ABC in 1971–72. "Rankin and Bass paid us a visit to get to know our personalities," Marlon remembers. "They were interested in what pets we owned and they observed the way we moved, and they wanted to know all about our likes and dislikes. We watched the show sometimes, but now my grandkids watch it on DVD."

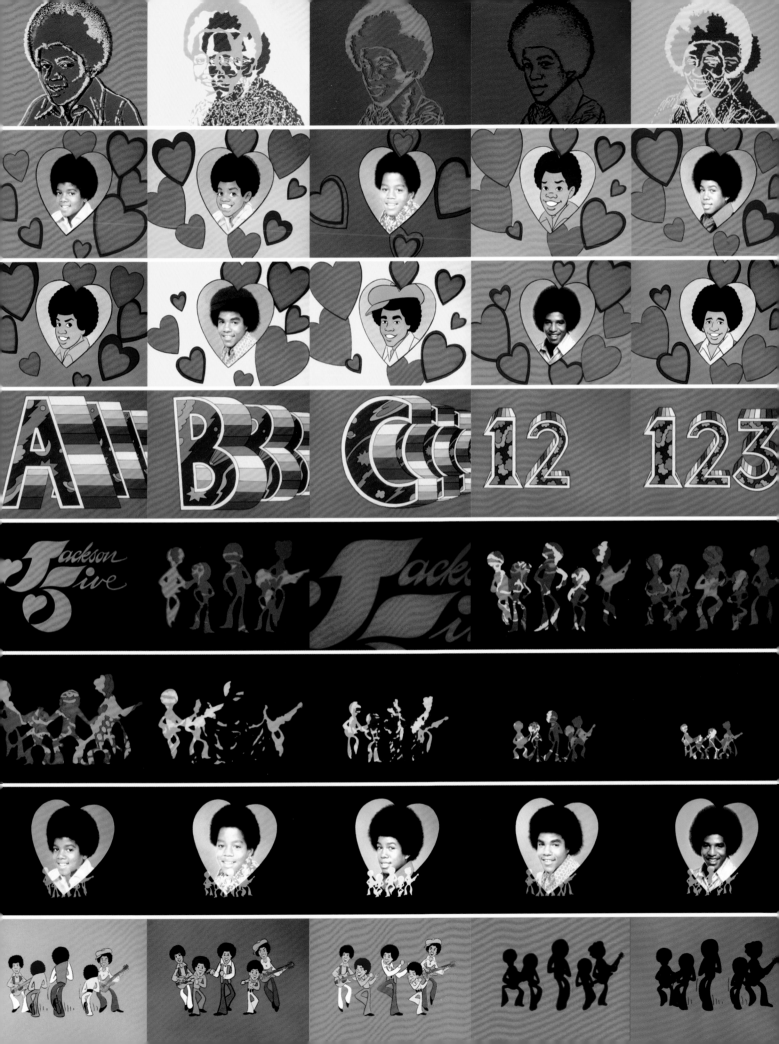

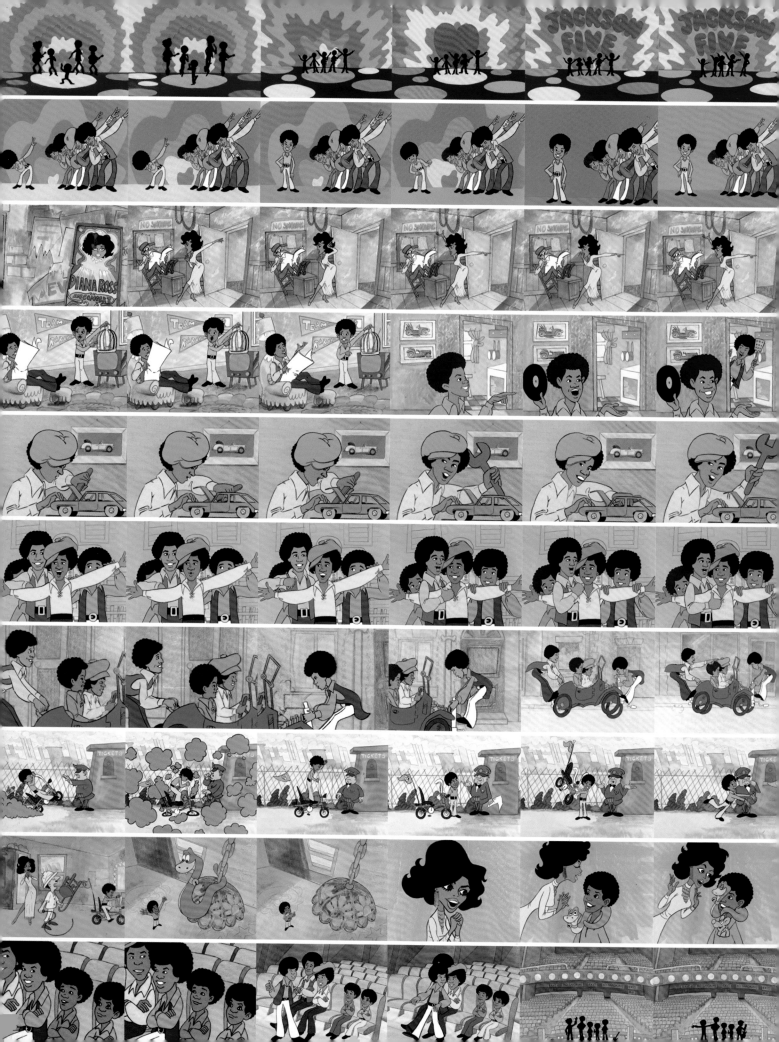

"**IT WAS THE FIRST SERIES FOR YOUNG PEOPLE ABOUT A GROUP OF BLACK PEOPLE, AND I FELT IT WAS VERY IMPORTANT TO SHOW THEM IN A CREATIVE WAY, TO SHOW HOW THEY SOLVED THEIR PROBLEMS WITH MUSIC AND INTELLIGENTLY, AND NOT BY VIOLENCE.**"

OPPOSITE The first episode of *Jackson 5ive* guest-starred Diana Ross, who provided her own voice. She also sang "My Place" from her album *Everything Is Everything*.
OVERLEAF The Jacksons were too busy recording and touring to provide their own voices for the series. Donald Fullilove was in the seventh grade when he was cast as Michael, and it was his first professional job. "I was a big fan of the group even before I did the show," he says. "I used to practice doing Michael's voice just in case his voice would give out during a show and they would need me to fill in."

ABOVE AND OPPOSITE Did the Jackson 5 enjoy being photographed? "Not really," Jackie admits. "But people always wanted to look at pictures of us. When you're an entertainer or a celebrity, you have to. If you want to be on magazine covers or do interviews where they run your photo, it's something you must do."

ABOVE Seen unfolded here, this Jackson 5 souvenir was distributed to fans. It included photographs from the television special *Goin' Back To Indiana*. **OPPOSITE** The names of the individual brothers form the number "5" on this promotional flyer for the *Jackson 5ive* animated series. **OVERLEAF** The Jacksons are one of the most photographed and well-documented families in the modern music era, as evidenced by this collage of articles, photographs, album covers, and memorabilia.

THE JACKSON 5

ELLEN MOTOVILOFF

T 2014

Jackson Five
ACTION GAME
For 3 or 4 players — Ages 5 through adult
* DECK OF JUMBO CARDS
* JACKSON 5 COINS
* SCORECARD
* MARKERS
As seen on the ABC-TV cartoon series

JACKIE TITO JERMAINE MARLON MICHAEL

No. 5000
©1972 SHINDANA TOYS
Div. of Operation Bootstrap, Inc.

A New Fun-And-Action Game For The Whole Family

Psst...Have I got a surprise for You
Turn to page

16
What do I talk about on the phone?
Turn to page 12 and listen in!

Shady Grove
Music Theatre
JACKSON FIVE

"J5 INVITE YOU "PUT YOURSELF IN OUR FAMILY CHRISTMAS PICTURE!"

The Jackson 5 in Paris

Get it together with the Jackson 5

Enter the J-5 $15,000 Get It Together Scholarship Contest.

JACKSON FIVE ZIP A DEE DOO DAH

AN EVENING WITH
Danny O'Donovan Presents
Jackson 5
And Supporting Artists
SUNDAY 12th NOVEMBER
1 SHOW: 7:00pm
Empire Pool, Wembley

THERE'S ONLY ONE PEARL... AND THAT'S MAMA'S!

YOUR MAIN SQUEEZE— IS IT JERMAINE, MICHAEL OR MARLON?

APRIL 1971 VOL 3 NO 1
SOUL ILLUSTRATED
2nd ANNIVERSARY ISSUE
THE JACKSON FIVE • ROBERTA FLACK /JIMI HENDRIX /FLIP WILSON /B.B. KING/ ISAAC HAYES/ SMOKEY ROBINSON/FREDA PAYNE/MELVIN VAN PEEBLES AND MANY MORE.

THE JACKSON 5

"G

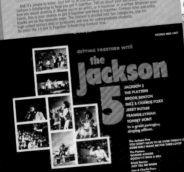

GETTING TOGETHER WITH
the Jackson 5
JACKSON 5
THE PLATTERS
BROOK BENTON
INEZ & CHARLIE FOXX
JERRY BUTLER
FRANKIE LYMAN
TOMMY HUNT
In a great swinging, singing album.

Jermaine Jackson
THAT'S HOW LOVE GOES
I LOST MY LOVE IN THE BIG CITY

The Best Of The Jackson 5

Jackson five

JACKIE

"Lookin' Through The Windows"

Jackson Five

OPPOSITE This group shot of the brothers was taken at the same
photo session as the individual images that appeared on *Lookin' Through
The Windows*, the seventh studio album by the Jackson 5 on Motown.
ABOVE *Lookin' Through The Windows* featured a title song written
by Clifton Davis. The first single to be released was a cover of Thurston
Harris's 1957 hit "Little Bitty Pretty One."

ABOVE AND OPPOSITE Most record labels used plain white sleeves to sheath and protect their LPs. In the late 1960s, Motown printed covers of current label releases on its sleeves. When *Lookin' Through The Windows* was released in 1972, the inner sleeve sported advertising for souvenirs that would appeal to Jackson 5 fans, including posters, photographs, and stickers.

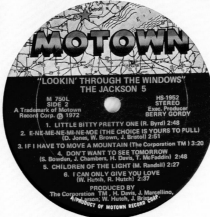

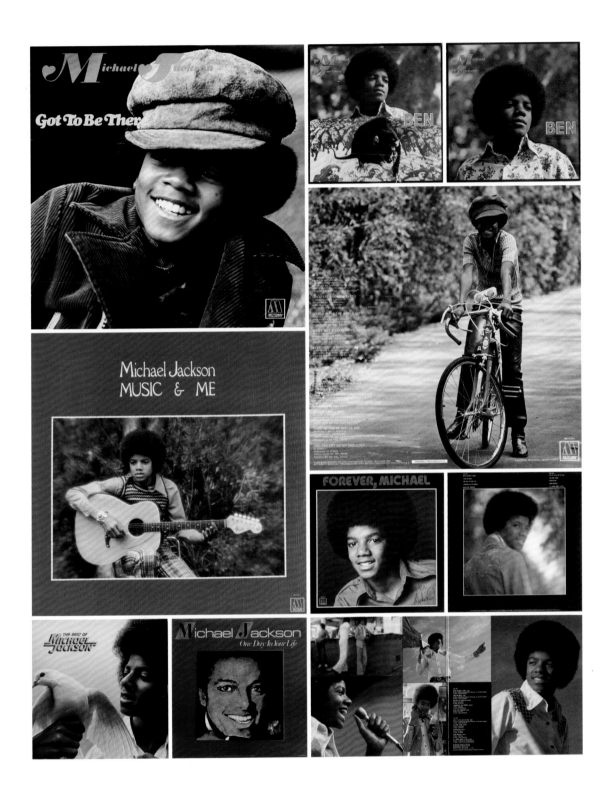

OPPOSITE Two years after the Jackson 5 debuted on the charts, Motown launched a solo career for Michael Jackson. **ABOVE** Starting with *Got To Be There* in 1972, the label released five Michael Jackson solo albums in the 1970s, including a greatest hits collection. In 1981, with Michael already signed to Epic, Motown released *One Day In Your Life*, which featured mid-1970s recordings from his tenure with the Detroit imprint.

Gladys Knight And The Pips: Soul Music Bonded By Blood

An Inside Look At Johnnie Taylor ✶ **Bobby Short: Long On Style**

Black Stars

A JOHNSON PUBLICATION   SEPTEMBER 1972   60¢

The Hopes
And Dreams Of
Diana Sands

Michael Jackson:
Too Much... Too Fast... Too Soon?

ABOVE Michael graced the cover of an early issue of *Black Stars*, a monthly magazine from the Johnson Publishing Company (which also published *Ebony* and *Jet*). *Black Stars* was published from 1971 to 1981. **OPPOSITE** This 1971 portrait of Michael didn't receive prominence until 2009, when it was used on the cover of the album *Pure Michael: Motown A Cappella*.

OPPOSITE Less than a year after Motown set Michael's solo career in motion, Jermaine also became a solo artist while remaining in the Jackson 5. His first single, "That's How Love Goes," only reached No. 46 on the *Billboard* Hot 100, but the follow-up, a remake of Shep & the Limelites' 1961 hit "Daddy's Home," peaked at No. 9. **ABOVE** Jermaine's first solo album debuted on the US album chart the week of August 12, 1972, and reached No. 27. **OVERLEAF** After Jermaine's eponymously titled debut, Motown released eight more solo albums by him, from 1973 to 1982. The most successful was *Let's Get Serious*, which peaked at No. 6 in 1980.

JERMAINE

COME INTO MY LIFE

MY NAME IS JERMAINE

Feel The Fire
JERMAINE
JACKSON

Jermaine Jackson
FRONTIERS

Part One

LET'S BE YOUNG TONIGHT
Don Daniels—Michael L. Smith
Jobete Music Co., Inc. (ASCAP) & Stone Diamond Music Corp. (BMI)
Arranged by Michael L. Smith
Produced by Michael L. Smith
Co-Produced by Don Daniels

FAITHFUL
Michael L. Smith—Don Daniels
Jobete Music Co., Inc. (ASCAP)
& Stone Diamond Music Corp., (BMI)
Arranged by Michael L. Smith
Produced by Michael L. Smith
Co-produced by Don Daniels

LOOK PAST MY LIFE
Terri McFaddin—Gregory Wright
Jobete Music Co., Inc. (ASCAP)
Produced & Arranged by Gregory Wright

BASS ODYSSEY
Gregory Wright
Jobete Music Co., Inc. (ASCAP)
Produced & Arranged by Gregory Wright

Part Two

WHO'S THAT LADY
Kenneth Lupper—Hubert Heard
Old Brompton Road (ASCAP) & Derglenn Publishing Co. (BMI)
Arranged by Kenny Lupper—William Bickelhaupt—Clay Drayton
Produced by Gwen Glenn Enterprises, Inc.

LOVELY YOU'RE THE ONE
Jeffrey Bowen—Truman Thomas—James Henry Ford
Stone Diamond Music Corp. (BMI)
Arranged by Truman Thomas
Produced by Jeffrey Bowen

STAY WITH ME
Michael B. Sutton—Brenda J. Sutton
Jobete Music Co., Inc. (ASCAP)
Arranged by Art Wright
Produced by Hal Davis & Michael B. Sutton

I JUST WANT TO TAKE THIS TIME
Eric Robinson—Victor Orsborn
Jobete Music Co., Inc. (ASCAP)
Arranged by Truman Thomas
Produced by Jeffrey Bowen

MY TOUCH OF MADNESS
Michael L. Smith
Jobete Music Co., Inc. (ASCAP)
Arranged by Michael L. Smith & William Goldstein
Produced by Michael L. Smith

Special thanks to Thelma Houston for vocal accompaniment

Assistant to the Executive Producer: Tony Jones

Recorded at Motown Recording Studios,
Hollywood, California 90028

Art Direction: Frank Mulvey
Photography by: Harry Langdon
Album Design: Craig Isobe

OPPOSITE On September 30, 1972, the brothers performed at the International Amphitheatre in Chicago as part of the PUSH (People United to Save Humanity) Expo, organized by Operation PUSH founder and civil rights leader Jesse Jackson. **ABOVE** This selection of sheet music includes eight of the Jackson 5's Motown hits and the Jacksons' first single on Epic, "Enjoy Yourself."

ABOVE The Jackson 5's 1972 tour of Europe took them to the Netherlands, Germany, France, and the UK. For the British leg of the tour, the brothers were gifted with personalized tote bags. **OPPOSITE** The brothers received a warm reception when they arrived in Europe for their first international tour. **OVERLEAF** These candid shots of the Jacksons were taken in the UK on October 31, 1972, one day after their Royal Variety Performance at the London Palladium and two days before they kicked off their European Tour.

2875-A1   2875-A2   2875-A3

A5   A6   A7

A9   A10   A11

2875-E2   2875-E3

"ONE MINUTE I WAS IN SCHOOL STUDYING BRITISH HISTORY. THE NEXT THING I KNOW, THE QUEEN IS ASKING US TO COME AND PERFORM. WE WERE TOLD HOW TO BEHAVE IN FRONT OF ROYALTY. YOU DON'T TALK TO THEM. YOU WAIT FOR THEM TO TALK TO YOU. THERE WERE SO MANY RULES."

OPPOSITE The Jackson 5 performed for Queen Elizabeth, the Queen Mother at the Royal Variety Performance on October 30, 1972. The celebrity line-up at the Palladium in London included Elton John, Jack Jones, comedian Rod Hull (and his puppet Emu), and British television stars Mike Yarwood and Ken Dodd.

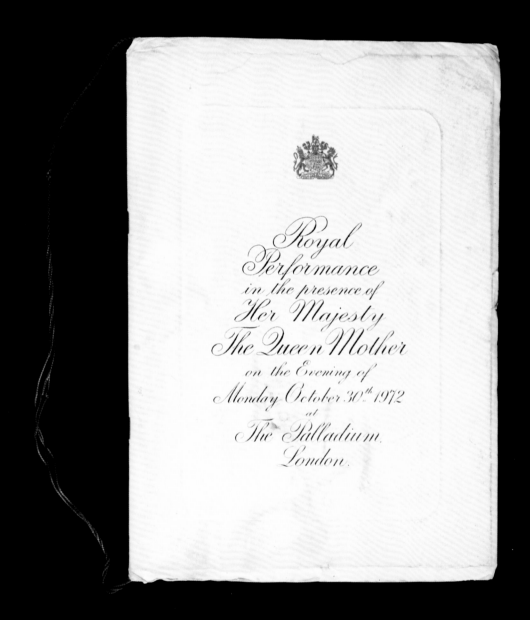

Royal Performance in the presence of Her Majesty The Queen Mother on the Evening of Monday October 30th 1972 at The Palladium, London.

ABOVE It was an honor to be invited to sing at the Royal Variety Performance in London, an annual event that dates back to 1912. In 1972, the Jackson 5 performed on a bill that featured stars such as Danny La Rue, Liberace, and Carol Channing.
OPPOSITE At least one member of the Royal Family is always present at the Royal Variety Performance. The Jackson 5 sang for Queen Elizabeth, the Queen Mother and were introduced to her backstage.

ABOVE AND OPPOSITE During their visit to the UK, the brothers enjoyed some periods of relaxation between performances. They also found time to shop and to meet fans.

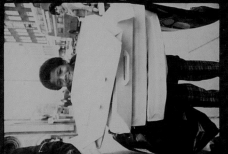

"WE WERE MOBBED BY 10,000 FANS AT THE AIRPORT...WE MADE IT INTO OUR CAR AND FANS WERE CHASING US DOWN THE ROAD. AS EXCITING AS IT ALL SOUNDS, IT WAS QUITE FRIGHTENING. WE WERE IN LONDON FOR OUR FIRST CONCERT ABROAD."

OPPOSITE Being famous didn't exempt the brothers from jet lag, and here they catch up on sleep during a drive through London. **OVERLEAF** Three days after their appearance at the Royal Variety Performance in London, Michael, Jermaine, Tito, Marlon, and Jackie kicked off their first European tour in the Netherlands, at the famed Concertgebouw in Amsterdam. The tour included stops in Germany and France before the group returned to the UK for shows in Birmingham, Manchester, Liverpool, and London.

OPPOSITE Work was constant for the Jackson 5. They spent many hours rehearsing their music and perfecting their craft. **ABOVE** Members of the Jackson family appeared on the cover of *Jet* magazine numerous times. Michael featured on the cover some forty times, as of the magazine's fiftieth anniversary in 2001, more than any other person. In second place was Muhammad Ali, with thirty-seven covers. **OVERLEAF** A rare photograph of Randy with his five older brothers. As the youngest brother, he traveled with his family and sometimes appeared on stage with them, but didn't officially join the group until after their Motown years.

ABOVE General Foods Corporation engaged the Jackson 5 as spokespersons for its Post cereal line, which included Super Sugar Crisp. In 1972, five different types of cereal featured a cardboard record that could be cut out from the back of the box. Although five songs were listed, only one appeared on each "flexi-disc." Some of the tunes available were "Never Can Say Goodbye," "I'll Bet You," and "Darling Dear." **OPPOSITE** Who better to film a commercial for Post's Alpha-Bits than the group that recorded "ABC"? The brothers shot these scenes with giant Alpha-Bits letters in Southern California's Griffith Park. "We had to eat the cereal as part of the commercial so they could show the letters floating in a bowl of milk," says Jackie. "I had a hard time with it because I don't like milk. I've always eaten my cereal dry; I still do today. Jermaine eats his cereal with apple juice. He loves it."

ABOVE AND OPPOSITE The Jackson 5 graced the cover of the very first issue of *Right On!* in 1972. The monthly magazine was published by the Laufer Company, whose portfolio also included the popular teen magazine *Tiger Beat*. Throughout the 1970s, the Jacksons appeared on more *Right On!* covers than any other artist.

ABOVE AND OPPOSITE In the backyard at the family home in Encino, California, youngest brother Randy
was included in the photo shoot, even though he wasn't a member of the group yet, and Joe joined his six sons, too.

ABOVE Jackie was the third member of the Jackson 5 to release a solo album. The LP featured original songs and also cover versions of the Delfonics' "Didn't I (Blow Your Mind This Time)" and the Miracles' "Bad Girl." **OPPOSITE** After owning a Datsun 240Z and a Z28 Camaro, Jackie bought a De Tomaso Pantera. "I took the Pantera to George Barris and he customized the whole car for me. He put pipes coming out the side. I had a sunroof and silver metal in the back." **OVERLEAF** The family home in Encino was a far cry from the two-bedroom house in Gary, Indiana. It served as a retreat from the world for the Jackson 5, where the brothers could relax by the swimming pool and play backyard sports.

ABOVE During their first tour of Europe, the Jackson 5 dropped by the BBC Studios to appear on *Top of the Pops*. The brothers sang Michael's solo hit "Rockin' Robin."

ABOVE Photographer Frank Carroll shot these pictures of the Jackson 5 on the set of *The Flip Wilson Show* at the NBC studios in Burbank, California.

ABOVE AND OPPOSITE Before the Jacksons became famous, the biggest cities they had visited were Chicago and New York. In the spring of 1973, they crossed the Pacific to begin their first tour of Japan, which included playing live shows in Tokyo, Hiroshima, and Osaka. Although Randy wasn't an official member of the group, he joined his brothers on the tour. "We thought the audiences in Japan didn't like us," says Tito. "They didn't show any reaction during the songs. But after each song, they all started applauding at the same time and they all stopped at the same time, waiting for the next song. That was unusual for us."

SWX-6024

IN JAPAN! JACKSON 5

ABOVE *In Japan!* was a live album recorded in 1973. It was released exclusively in Japan in October 1973 and wasn't available elsewhere until 1986, when it was issued in the UK. *In Japan!* was finally released in the USA as a limited edition CD in October 2004.

IN JAPAN! JACKSON 5

ABOVE In addition to the usual Jackson 5 hits and solo performances by Michael and Jermaine, *In Japan!* included cover versions of Stevie Wonder's "Superstition," the Temptations' "Papa Was A Rollin' Stone," and Marvin Gaye's "Ain't That Peculiar." **PAGES 136–139** Like many families, the Jacksons kept scrapbooks of their travels.

OPPOSITE Four years after first performing at the Forum in Inglewood, California, as part of a Diana Ross & the Supremes show, the brothers returned to the venue. **ABOVE** Michael and the Jackson 5 in concert at the Forum on August 26, 1973.

ABOVE The Jackson 5 were guests on *The Bob Hope Show* on September 26, 1973, along with Ann-Margret, John Denver, and tennis player Bobby Riggs.

ABOVE The Jackson 5 performed two songs—"Get It Together" and "Dancing Machine"—on the Bob Hope special, recorded at NBC in Burbank, California.

THE JACKSON FIVE WINS NEW ACCLAIM ON TOUR OF AFRICA

MARCH 7, 1974/50¢ | A JOHNSON PUBLICATION

JET

JOSEPH JACKSON

MICHAEL JACKSON

JACKIE JACKSON

TITO JACKSON

MARLON JACKSON

RANDY JACKSON

JERMAINE JACKSON

ABOVE The cover story for the March 7, 1974 issue of *Jet* was about the Jackson 5's first trip to Africa. The brothers performed three shows in Dakar, Senegal, on February 1, 2, and 3, 1974.

ABOVE *Jet* continued its frequent coverage of the Jackson 5 with a cover story in the
August 1, 1974 issue about their residency at the original MGM Grand Hotel, Las Vegas.
They played thirty-five shows, which also featured siblings LaToya, Randy, and Janet.

ABOVE Irish photographer Fin Costello captured the moment Michael encountered a friendly dove at an outdoor zoo in Jamaica in 1975. **OPPOSITE** Costello also took this photograph of the Jackson 5 during their short trip to Jamaica. He began his career as a sports photographer in 1966, but five years later started to take pictures of musicians, eventually working with Deep Purple, Pink Floyd, Duran Duran, Aerosmith, Ozzy Osbourne, the Police, the Rolling Stones, Jimi Hendrix, and Kiss.

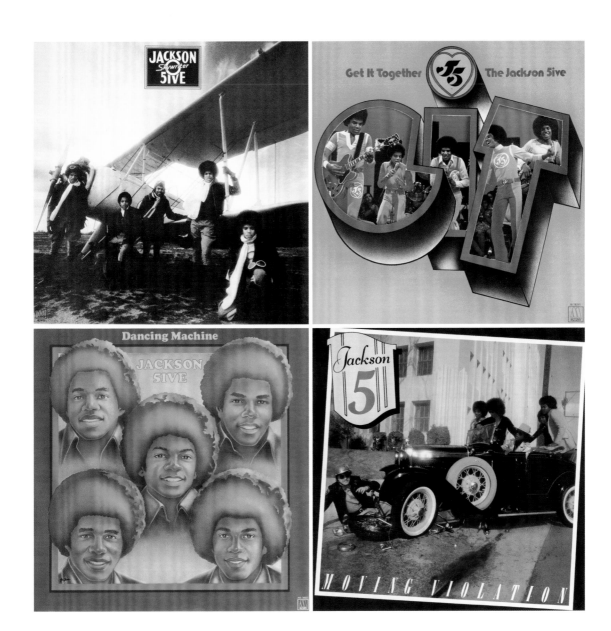

OPPOSITE (L to R) Tito, Jackie, Michael, Jermaine, and Marlon posed for a photograph in their colorful tuxedos before performing at the National Stadium in Kingston, Jamaica. **ABOVE** The final four Jackson 5 studio albums on Motown were *Skywriter* (1973), *Get It Together* (1973), *Dancing Machine* (1974), and *Moving Violation* (1975). **OVERLEAF** The Jackson 5 performed only one show at the National Stadium in Kingston, Jamaica, in March 1975. Bob Marley and the Wailers were also on the bill, and a local newspaper reported that the disorganized show ended at 4 o'clock in the morning.

"COMPARED TO WHAT WENT ON ON TUESDAY NIGHT, THE ROLLING STONES SHOW WAS A SQUARE DANCE AND THE ELVIS PRESLEY CONCERT WAS A TEA PARTY. NOBODY CAN COME CLOSE TO THE JACKSON 5 IN TURNING A CROWD INTO A SQUIRMING SHRIEKING MOB."

OVERLEAF The Jacksons spent time in Jamaica with Bob Marley and his family. "He was an amazing guy who stood for peace and equality and his songs resonated around the world," says Jackie. "We did a show in Jamaica, and he opened up for us.... After the concert, he invited us to his home. He fixed dinner for us and we had a great time."

AN EPIC DECISION.

UNHAPPY AT MOTOWN, THE GROUP SIGNS WITH EPIC RECORDS. JERMAINE LEAVES THE JACKSON 5 AND STAYS WITH BERRY GORDY'S LABEL. YOUNGEST BROTHER RANDY, WHO HAS ALWAYS WANTED TO MAKE MUSIC WITH HIS BROTHERS, IS OFFICIALLY INVITED TO JOIN THE GROUP, WHICH IS NOW KNOWN AS THE JACKSONS. MICHAEL'S SOLO CAREER ON THE EPIC LABEL FLOURISHES WITH *OFF THE WALL* FOLLOWED BY THE BIGGEST-SELLING ALBUM OF ALL TIME, *THRILLER*.

THE JACKSON FAMILY was living in a house rented for them by Motown in Beverly Hills when they decided to invest in a home of their own. A real estate agent showed Katherine Jackson a home in Bel Air and another property in Encino, located in the San Fernando Valley. Bel Air is one of Los Angeles's more upscale neighborhoods, and the real estate agent expected the family to purchase a home there. Katherine says they preferred the Encino home for its eighteen fruit trees, expansive land, and basketball court. The Jacksons paid $140,000 for the property and moved into their new home on May 5, 1971. An actress who appeared in one of the most beloved motion pictures of all time offered a different version of why the family settled in Encino. Charmian Carr played the oldest von Trapp child, Liesl, in the 1965 film *The Sound of Music*.

CHARMIAN CARR: Michael read in the newspaper that Liesl from *The Sound of Music* had moved to Encino after she got married. He said to his mother, "Liesl lives in Encino, why don't we move there?" And that's how Michael and his family ended up living down the street from me.

After giving up her acting career to devote time to her family, Carr became an interior designer. Years later, when Michael was building his own home, his contractor suggested a meeting with Carr.

CHARMIAN CARR: Michael was a huge fan of *The Sound of Music* and he always used to ask me about making the film. He wanted his home to have the same feel as Disneyland—he even wanted one room to resemble the "Pirates of the Caribbean" ride—so he asked me to go to the theme park with him, many times. He would dress up in disguise so no one would know it was him, although people always did.

Michael may have wanted to move to Encino to borrow a cup of sugar from Liesl, but his brothers didn't feel the same way.

TITO JACKSON: I didn't want to move to the Valley because I thought it was too hot. After a while, we got used to the summer heat; also we were still touring so we didn't have to be in the Valley for the entire summer. Living in Hollywood and then Beverly Hills, we were used to walking down Sunset Boulevard or hanging out in West Hollywood Park. We couldn't do that in Encino, although eventually we discovered Balboa Park.

MARLON JACKSON: I didn't know anything about Encino. We heard that a lot of people lived there, like Chuck Connors from *The Rifleman*. We had a long driveway, and when we weren't in the studio we spent a lot of time playing basketball or swimming in our pool.

One day the gates to the Encino compound opened to admit a famous guest, who slowly drove down the driveway in her car.

JACKIE JACKSON: Who was it? Michael's good friend Jane Fonda. I walked over and said hello. She hugged all of us and suddenly we started playing basketball. She had her tennis shoes on and we played for hours until she said, "Let's go get something to drink. Let's get a six pack of beer." All five of us piled into the car with her and we drove down the boulevard to a little store on Kester and picked up two six packs of beer. My brothers didn't drink any of it. I was drinking the beer with her and I got all messed up because I wasn't a drinker at all. But I drank beer with Jane Fonda because it was sociable and I had a good time with her. She's a wonderful friend, still today. She's the nicest person I ever met, so down to earth. No one would ever believe that she came over and played basketball and hung out with us, but that's what she did. I'll never forget that.

The same year that the family bought the Encino property, Michael and Marlon spent a couple of nights away from home—in hospital.

MARLON: Michael and I had our tonsils out at the same time. We were in the same room at the hospital and Diana Ross paid us a visit. When we came home, the radio was on and we heard a song that sounded just like "I Want You Back." We said, "Hey, somebody's trying to sound like us." We found out later that the song had been written for us, but Motown turned it down because they had their own writers. The song was "One Bad Apple" by the Osmonds and it was a hit record for them. It put them on the map.

TITO: I thought "One Bad Apple" was a rip-off of us. The Osmonds had been singing with Andy Williams, doing country music and barbershop-type songs. But they were a good group. They were a solid band. They were our first rivals, and after them came the DeFrancos. We were friends with the

Osmonds. We played sports together and had a lot of fun. Donny has always been a cool guy and so have his brothers.

DONNY OSMOND: The first time I met Michael, we were performing in Toronto at the Canadian National Exhibition in 1971. The Jackson 5 performed the day after us. The stadium was sold out and I looked stage right and there was Michael, peeking around the curtain watching us. After the show, we all went back to our hotel. The two families got together, and my mom and dad were sitting on the sofa with Joe and Katherine, talking business. Marie was talking with the Jackson girls. All Michael and I wanted to do was go off and play with our toys. When "One Bad Apple" came out, everybody said we were copying the Jackson 5. But Joe told my father he used to make his boys watch us on *The Andy Williams Show*, and he would tell them, "I want you guys to do that."

"One Bad Apple" topped the *Billboard* Hot 100 four months after "I'll Be There." Both songs had five-week reigns. Perhaps Motown made a mistake not letting the Jackson 5 record the song; it could have been their fifth consecutive No. 1.

JACKIE: "One Bad Apple" was a great song but Berry had his own writers and producers.

It's true. Motown's roster of in-house writers and producers was responsible for a very long honor roll of hits. It is the reason why many—but not all—of the Motown artists did not write and produce themselves, apart from songwriter/producers such as Smokey Robinson, Stevie Wonder, and Marvin Gaye. As the Jackson 5 matured they expressed a desire to write and produce themselves, but Motown said no. The label didn't need the Jackson brothers to write their own material when they had dozens of proven hit-making composers and producers.

Their desire to write their own material along with their father's concern that Motown's royalty rate on record sales was too low were the main reasons the group considered leaving Motown when their seven-year contract was up.

The Jacksons were not the only artists to think about exiting the label and signing with another company. Mary Wells departed in the 1960s after she had a No. 1 Motown single with "My Guy." The Four Tops signed with ABC Records in 1972, and a year later Gladys Knight & the Pips moved to Buddah. In 1974, Martha Reeves signed with MCA (and later Arista). The Temptations left briefly for Atlantic in 1977, and then former Temptations Eddie Kendricks and David Ruffin found new homes at Arista and Warner Brothers, respectively. Later, Diana Ross split for RCA in the USA and EMI outside of North America, and Marvin Gaye joined the Columbia roster.

It wasn't that Motown was failing the Jackson 5. True, their chart fortunes were a bit diminished after "Never Can Say Goodbye," and only two more singles reached the Top 10 in the USA: "Sugar Daddy" (No. 10 in 1972) and "Dancing Machine" (No. 2 in 1974). But *Billboard*'s R&B charts showed a different view. There, all seventeen of the quintet's Motown singles achieved Top 10 status, which is one of the longest runs of consecutive Top 10 hits in the chart's history.

It was a slightly different story in the UK, where the first four Motown singles all made the Top 10, but none of them went to No. 1. "I Want You Back" peaked at No. 2, followed by "ABC" (No. 8), "The Love You Save" (No. 7), and "I'll Be There" (No. 4). There were two more Top 10 hits in the UK: "Lookin' Through The Windows" (No. 9) and a cover of Jackson Browne's "Doctor My Eyes" (No. 9).

Back in the USA, Motown launched solo careers for three of the Jacksons. Michael was recording on his own as early as 1971, when "Got To Be There" peaked at No. 4. It was followed by a remake of Bobby Day's 1958 hit "Rockin' Robin," which went to No. 2. A few months later, Michael's recording of the title song from the film *Ben* was sitting on top of the *Billboard* Hot 100.

In *Moonwalk* Michael wrote, "It was Berry Gordy's idea that I should do a solo recording and so I became one of the first people in a Motown group to really step out. Berry also said he thought I should record my own album.... When I did, I realized he was right."

A year after Michael's first single on his own, Jermaine's "That's How Love Goes" kicked off his solo career. Although that first single barely cracked the Top 50, the follow-up, a remake of Shep & the Limelites' 1961 hit "Daddy's Home," sailed to No. 9. Jermaine went to No. 9 again with an original "Let's Get Serious," cowritten and produced by Stevie Wonder.

Jermaine wrote in his book *You Are Not Alone: Michael, Through a Brother's Eyes,* "We never forgot that the group came first. The Jackson 5 was our security; the solo projects were our experimental adventures."

In 1973, Motown issued a solo album by the oldest Jackson brother.

JACKIE: Berry told me, "You're going to make a solo album," and Fonce Mizell and Freddie Perren also told me I was going to make a solo album. I guess it was because the fans wanted me to make one, so I did. People come up to me today and tell me about the songs they like on the record, and it always surprises me. I don't think about the solo album because I'm so hung up on all the great music that we did as the Jacksons, or Michael's music or Janet's music. I'm happy to hear that people still remember the songs on my solo album. I was singing more in a falsetto voice with a lot of strings. It was the type of music that fit my audience—older people—since I was a little older than my brothers. I love the album but I don't play it very much. There's a song called "Love Don't Want To Leave," which was one of my favorites. It is one that everybody loved. It was difficult to make the solo album because I had been around my brothers and was in the studio with them all of my life. To do something on my own was exciting, but I like to sing with my brothers. It's not about me having a solo album. It's about the Jackson 5 and the Jacksons.

While still signed to Motown, the Jackson 5 had a residency at the original MGM Grand Hotel in Las Vegas. But it wasn't only the Jackson 5—their other four siblings also appeared on stage with them. The two youngest, Janet and Randy, duetted on Mickey & Sylvia's 1957 classic "Love Is Strange." One of the most memorable moments of the show was when seven-year-old Janet sauntered over to Randy with a boa wrapped around her neck and said, doing her best Mae West impression, "Why don't you come up and see me sometime?"

JACKIE: We really enjoyed doing those shows. We did two shows a day. Frank Gorshin was our opening act. Those were fun times.

Tito was the first Jackson brother to wed. He and his bride, Dee Dee, tied the knot in June 1972. A year later, Jermaine broke the news to his family that he was also getting

married—to Hazel Gordy, daughter of Berry Gordy. The wedding took place on December 15, 1973, at the Beverly Hills Hotel. *Ebony* magazine called it the "wedding of the century."

Jermaine wrote in his book that he had nothing to say about the ceremony's theme or decadence. "The guest list was a Who's Who of the music industry and the grand theme a winter wonderland...with 175 white doves, artificial snow, and Smokey Robinson singing "Starting Here And Now," a song written especially for us." The wedding was grander than Tito's, but then Jermaine was marrying the boss's daughter.

On June 30, 1975, the Jackson brothers held a press conference to announce that they were leaving Motown and signing with CBS, effective on March 10, 1976. Their new home would be Epic Records, and they would be receiving a larger share of royalties and would be involved in writing their own material. But those weren't the only changes. Jermaine made the difficult decision not to join his siblings at Epic. He was going to remain with Motown and he was dropping out of the Jackson 5.

JACKIE: He was married to Hazel, but Hazel wanted him to go with his brothers. She told him, "Just because you're married to me should have nothing to do with it. You should be with your brothers." But he decided that he wanted to stay, and that's what he wanted to do.

Jermaine's decision had a huge impact on Michael. "I clearly remember the first show we did without him, because it was so painful for me," he wrote in *Moonwalk*. "Since my earliest days on the stage—and even in our rehearsals in our Gary living room—Jermaine stood at my left with his bass. I *depended* on being next to Jermaine. And when I did that first show without him there, with no one next to me, I felt totally naked on stage for the first time in my life. So we worked harder to compensate for the loss of one of our shining stars, Jermaine."

MARLON: I was too young to realize it was a big deal to leave Motown. We came to Motown with the name Jackson 5 and I thought we should walk away with it. But they kept it, and that's why we changed it to the Jacksons. Emotionally, it was tough to leave. I really appreciated Motown. Berry gave us our start. It was an investment for him and

it was a risky investment, but it paid off. Still, he was the one who took the risk and I appreciate that.

Although the brothers could no longer call themselves the Jackson 5, there were still five Jacksons. As Jermaine stepped out, youngest brother Randy was finally invited to join the group.

JACKIE: During the Motown years, whenever we left to go on the road, we'd have to leave Randy behind. He thought he was ready to come with us. We knew he had the talent, but we felt he wasn't ready to join the group yet. We'd be going out of the gates of our home in Encino, and we'd look back and see him standing in the driveway crying. He was always rehearsing with us, but he didn't travel with us. When we told him he was joining the group, he was so excited. Tears were coming out of his eyes. He was ready, and we wanted the world to see what this little guy could do, because he could really play.

TITO: It was a new life and a new company, a much bigger company. We were going to be working with Kenny Gamble and Leon Huff, so I felt safe because I knew the hits that they had produced in the past.

Gamble and Huff were successful writers and producers who had been charting since 1964. They had created the "The Sound of Philadelphia," and their single "TSOP" was the first television theme song to reach No. 1. Their first successful act was the Intruders, who scored hits with songs such as "Together" and "Cowboys To Girls." They also produced artists including Jerry Butler, Dusty Springfield, Wilson Pickett, Archie Bell & the Drells, and Joe Simon, before forming their own Philadelphia International label and signing artists such as the O'Jays, the Three Degrees, Billy Paul, Lou Rawls, and Harold Melvin & the Blue Notes.

TITO: Once Gamble and Huff got us into the studio, the album didn't take very long to put together. We drove to Philadelphia and stayed in a hotel, and two weeks later we had the album done. They were great producers to work with and had everything ready. They knew what they wanted us to sing and do, and worked with us before we went into the studio.

The Jackson 5's final Motown single to chart on the *Billboard* Hot 100 was a remake of Diana Ross & the Supremes' song "Forever Came Today." Written by three of the architects of the Motown sound—Eddie Holland, Lamont Dozier, and Brian Holland—the Jackson 5's version was produced by Brian Holland and marked Brian and Eddie's return to Berry Gordy's company after an absence of a few years.

JACKIE: We loved that song and it was a dream come true to work with those guys. They were just incredible. To be in the presence of [Brian and Eddie] was amazing. They had so many other hits with Motown and were very professional. They came up with a gospel kind of groove. In the rehearsal hall, the choreography was incredible. We made some great moves on that song.

"Forever Came Today" only peaked at No. 60, but it remains a part of the Jacksons' legacy and they still perform it live today. After the single fell off the *Billboard* Hot 100, the Jacksons didn't return to the chart until the debut of their first Epic single "Enjoy Yourself." Released with the logo of Gamble and Huff's Philadelphia International Records on the label, the 45 debuted on the Hot 100 the week of November 13, 1976, and went on to peak at No. 6. With the exception of "Dancing Machine," it was the Jacksons' only Top 10 single since "Sugar Daddy" in 1972.

MARLON: I take my hat off to Gamble and Huff. They wrote a bunch of hits before we worked with them, but when it was time for them to write for the Jacksons they came up with a different sound from what they normally wrote, even though the songs still had that Philadelphia feel and sound. They did some nice stuff and we had a great time with them.

It didn't take very long for the Jacksons to notice differences between Motown and their new label home.

TITO: Epic was such a large company; it was more of a business. It was just a record company, whereas Motown was a record company and a family. So it was different. If you wanted to see Berry Gordy, you didn't need an appointment. You could be down the hall working with Hal Davis, and if Berry was in his office you could go in and say hi. At Epic, that wasn't going to happen. You had to go through the secretaries. And usually they'd say, "Mr. [Walter] Yetnikoff is tied up right now."

After "Enjoy Yourself," Epic released the follow-up "Show You The Way To Go." Another Gamble and Huff composition, it went no higher than No. 28 on the *Billboard* Hot 100, but became the Jacksons' only No. 1 in the UK. The next single was "Goin' Places," the title song from the Jacksons' second album with Gamble and Huff. It peaked at No. 52.

TITO: I didn't think "Goin' Places" should be a single, but it was a fun song because it was about traveling and I think Kenny Gamble and Leon Huff wanted to encourage black people to travel more. They wanted to let them know about our experiences of all the places we had been and that it is important for people to travel and see other cultures, because the world is a big place.

For *Destiny*, their third Epic album, the Jacksons came under the aegis of Bobby Colomby, the vice president of Epic A&R. An original member of the group Blood, Sweat & Tears, Colomby was brought into the Epic fold by label president Ron Alexenburg in the summer of 1977.

BOBBY COLOMBY: It seemed clear that the record company had no interest in the Jacksons. Ron was getting ready to leave and they had no advocates left. Artists get deserted when people leave. Columbia had serious legacy acts such as Neil Diamond and Barbra Streisand and didn't really care about the Jacksons. I started to make calls to find a producer for them. I was a fan of the British band Heatwave and thought that style of music would work for them. Heatwave's producer was Barry Blue. He flew in from England and I met with him. There was a fellow in my department, Mike Atkinson, who was a sweet guy, but he had never been through the process of making a record. He was a promotion guy, a really good guy. One day he walked in and said he'd found a song. It was a record on Atco by Mick Jackson. I thought ["Blame It On The Boogie"] would be a smash for the Jacksons.

Colomby asked Michael and Randy if they could write original songs. "We try," Michael replied, "but they never use our songs." Then Colomby brought in pianist Greg Phillinganes to organize music for the Jacksons and to arrange their rhythm section. Phillinganes came to the Epic office and Colomby drove him to the Jacksons' home in Encino.

BOBBY COLOMBY: I hired an arranger, Clare Fischer, for "Blame It On The Boogie." Greg Phillinganes did the rhythm arrangement. I also booked the studio and hired engineer Don Murray. We were ready to go, but then Barry Blue said, "I don't want to do the record." So I told the group, "I'll let you produce." Saying the record was produced and written by the Jacksons would give them adult credibility. The first day in the studio, we recorded "Blame It On The Boogie" and "Push Me Away." On "Blame It On The Boogie," the chords had to sing; the harmonies were not their typical harmonies. I took a page from Roy Thomas Baker, who produced Queen. On "Bohemian Rhapsody," he had everyone sing the bass and everyone sing the treble. Some of the guys said, "That's not the way we record." But Michael was the greatest. He got it right away and was a joy to work with. It was his moment of maturity and I pushed him into writing. I figured they had "Blame It On The Boogie" and was sure that it was a hit. I was content they had that one in the bag, so I let them write everything else.

"Blame It On The Boogie" remains a fan favorite, but the single didn't do particularly well, peaking at No. 54. The follow-up did better. "Shake Your Body (Down To The Ground)" became the Jacksons' highest-charting single on Epic, at No. 7 in the USA.

BOBBY COLOMBY: Greg worked with Randy and Michael on "Shake Your Body (Down To The Ground)" and cut a twenty-minute track of one chord. I couldn't see doing twenty minutes of one chord, so I started adding stuff to make it less boring. I called [horn arranger] Tom Tom 84 because I was a big Earth, Wind & Fire fan. He filled in the holes. We added percussion and really put in the entire kitchen sink. Michael sang the verse, which was dissonant, but when the chorus hit, it was so pleasant. There's so much tension in the melody. It was a nice simple chorus. I knew I had to edit it down because it was long at over twenty minutes. We got it down to eight minutes for the album. No one had any interest in "Blame It On The Boogie" in the USA, but the promotion guy asked me for a three-minute version of "Shake Your Body" [for radio]. I took the album version and at 3:15 I started fading. We listened to it and suddenly I was hearing it as a 3:47 record. I looked at the promotion guy

and said, "This is a hit!" The energy of them singing, that's what got people. The fun of it.

TITO: "Shake Your Body" is cool because it was different and it was written completely by the brothers. It was a song that we pieced together, actually. We had the music and we went in the studio and started putting things together.

On March 25, 1983, the Jacksons took part in an historic Motown family reunion at the Pasadena Civic Auditorium in Southern California. Diana Ross & the Supremes, the Temptations, Marvin Gaye, the Four Tops, Stevie Wonder, the Miracles, Martha Reeves, Mary Wells, Junior Walker, Lionel Richie and the Commodores, and DeBarge were all there, too, for the taping of *Motown 25: Yesterday, Today, Forever*. The NBC special, which was seen by almost 34 million viewers on May 16, featured the Jackson 5 (including Randy and a returning Jermaine) singing a medley of "I Want You Back," "Never Can Say Goodbye," "The Love You Save," and "I'll Be There." Michael was hesitant about appearing on the special, but he responded to Berry Gordy's personal invitation with the request that he be allowed a solo spot. He performed the only non-Motown song on the show when he "moonwalked" to "Billie Jean."

MARLON: Doing that show with all of these artists who influenced the world was very special. It was an exploding combustion of energy. Backstage, Michael and I were hanging out in the dressing room with Diana Ross and Billy Dee Williams. I wasn't a Star Wars fan until recently, when I took my grandson to see one of the movies, so I didn't ask Billy about *The Empire Strikes Back* or *Return of the Jedi*.

TITO: Michael doing the moonwalk was a surprise to everyone. Michael was hot at that time, so everybody was gathered backstage around the monitors. We had seen the moonwalk many times, because we'd been around Michael his whole life. Marlon and the other brothers were able to do the moonwalk, too, but we never presented it or thought about putting it in the show like that. He used it brilliantly and it became a signature move for him.

Jermaine explained how he felt about reuniting with his siblings on stage in his book *You Are Not Alone: Michael, Through*

a Brother's Eyes. "Just the thought of performing again with the brothers elated me. For six years, I'd had a recurring dream that I was on stage with them and I was counting a song off in my head, just about to sing...and then I'd wake. My unconscious had teased me with that promise for too long. Now, it was going to be a reality and I couldn't wait."

Jermaine notes the perfect moment arrived when they all walked on stage as the original Jackson 5. "The magic and chemistry returned naturally. All that had altered was that we weren't kids anymore and, golly, we had fun that night. I was overcome with the sensation of 'we're back,' even if it was for only one night. I didn't care, because this was the moment that, in the back of my mind, I'd known would happen again. Poetically, when it was my part to sing on 'I'll Be There,' during the medley, my mic went out. Michael, alert to every beat, sensed it, saw my lips move with no sound, and scooted over to share his mic, putting his arm around me as I sang.... I think many people thought it was staged as we both leaned into his mic, but it was a technical glitch...and that image is one I treasure from a momentous night."

Michael also wrote about the *Motown 25* special in his book *Moonwalk*. "The night before the taping, I still had no idea what I was going to do with my solo number. So I went down to the kitchen of our house and played 'Billie Jean.' Loud. I was in there by myself, the night before the show, and I pretty much stood there and let the song tell me what to do. I kind of let the dance create itself. I really let it *talk* to me; I heard the beat come in and I took this spy's hat and started to pose and step, letting the rhythm create the moments.... I had been practicing the moonwalk for some time and it dawned on me in our kitchen that I would finally do the moonwalk in public on *Motown 25*."

Michael went on to explain that the day after the special aired, he received a phone call from his lifelong idol Fred Astaire, who told him, "You're a hell of a mover." Michael wrote, "It was the greatest compliment I had ever received in my life and the only one I had ever wanted to believe. For Fred Astaire to tell me that meant more than anything."

Michael's moonwalk was an unforgettable moment of television history, a star turn that put his *Thriller* album on course to become the best-selling album of all time.

ABOVE *Sepia* magazine, a rival to *Ebony*, was published from 1947 to 1983. The July 1976 issue presented the revised line-up of the Jacksons on the cover—minus Jermaine but with the addition of Randy—five months before the group issued its first album on the Epic label. **OPPOSITE** This photo shoot at a pool featured the post-Motown roster of Jacksons: Jackie, Tito, Marlon, Michael, and Randy.

JACKIE JACKSON:

"WHEN WE SIGNED WITH EPIC AND JERMAINE LEFT THE GROUP, IT HURT US, BECAUSE ONE OF OUR BROTHERS WAS STAYING AT MOTOWN. HE HAD HIS OWN REASONS WHY HE WANTED TO STAY. I CAN'T KNOCK HIM FOR THAT."

OPPOSITE This November 1978 television special was a family affair, featuring sisters LaToya, Janet, and Rebbie along with their famous brothers. Janet, the youngest Jackson sibling, was only twelve years old.

ABOVE *The Jacksons* was the group's first album for Epic Records. Produced by the famed team of Kenny Gamble and Leon Huff, the LP shared a logo with their Philadelphia International imprint. The 1976 release yielded two hit singles—"Enjoy Yourself" and "Show You The Way To Go"—and included two songs written by the Jacksons: "Style Of Life" and "Blues Away."

ABOVE The Jacksons' second album for Epic on the Philadelphia International imprint—*Goin' Places*—was also produced by Kenny Gamble and Leon Huff. The title track from the LP was the only single to be a hit in the USA.

OPPOSITE AND ABOVE The Jacksons visited London after signing with Epic Records, and photographer Tom Sheehan was assigned to shoot pictures all around the city. "CBS promo legend Judd Lander suggested showing the Jacksons all the usual tourist sites," Sheehan recalls. "We were in two limos and we took in all the London landmarks, including Big Ben, the Tower of London, No. 10 Downing Street (back in the days when you could walk right up to the door), and Buckingham Palace. We ended up at the Hammersmith Odeon, where they were going to do a show. At each location we just hopped out, took a few shots, and rolled on to the next location. It wasn't a photo session, more like taking holiday snaps." The group also visited Glasgow, where they performed in front of the Queen and the Duke of Edinburgh at the Kings Theatre on May 17, 1977 as part of the Royal Command Performance celebrating the Queen's Silver Jubilee. They were photographed meeting the royal couple (above, top), along with British and international stars including Ronnie Corbett, Frankie Howerd, and Dolly Parton.

ABOVE While in London for their performance at the Hammersmith Odeon, the Jacksons rehearsed for an appearance on a British television show.

ABOVE On May 24, 1977, the Jacksons performed on stage at the
Hammersmith Odeon in West London to a full house.

SIDE ONE
Blame It On The Boogie • Push Me Away • Things I Do For You • Shake Your Body (Down To The Ground)
SIDE TWO
Destiny • Bless His Soul • All Night Dancin' • That's What You Get (For Being Polite)
"Through the ages, the peacock has been honored and praised for its attractive, illustrious beauty.
Of all the bird family, the peacock is the only bird that integrates all colors into one, and displays this radiance of fire only when in love."
"We, like the peacock, try to integrate all races into one through the love of music."
— Michael and Jackie Jackson For Peacock Productions

STEREO
Epic
EPC 83200

Produced and Written by The Jacksons*
Executive Producers: Bobby Colomby and Mike Atkinson • Engineered by Peter Granet and Don Murray
Recorded at Cherokee Recording Studios, Total Experience, Heiders/Filmways, Record Plant and Dawnbreakers, Los Angeles, California
Mixed at Westlake Audio and Producers Workshop, Los Angeles, California
Management: Weisner/DeMann Entertainment, Inc. and Joe Jackson
*Except 'Blame It On The Boogie'
℗ 1978 CBS Inc./© 1978 CBS Inc.
Epic is a Registered Trademark of CBS Inc.
WARNING – Copyright subsists in all CBS recordings. Any unauthorised broadcasting, public performance, copying or re-recording in any manner whatsoever will constitute infringement
of such copyright. Licences for the use of records for public performance may be obtained from Phonographic Performance Ltd., Ganton House, 14—22 Ganton Street, London W.1.
Interpak I by Shorewood Packaging Co. Ltd., England

PREVIOUS The line-up during the Epic years was (L to R) Jackie, Marlon, Randy, Tito, and Michael.
ABOVE *Destiny* was the third Jacksons album on the Epic label. For the first time, the brothers produced
their own LP, working with Epic A&R executive Bobby Colomby. The first single, "Blame It On The Boogie,"
was issued in August 1978, two months before the album. It was a mid-charter, but the follow-up,
"Shake Your Body (Down To The Ground)," returned the brothers to the Top 10.

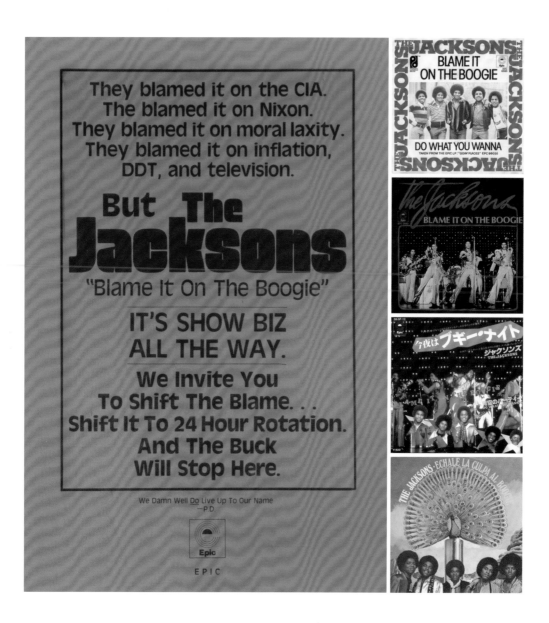

ABOVE LEFT This trade advertisement for the first single from the *Destiny* album, "Blame It On The Boogie," was released in 1978. Earlier that year, the original version of the song, by British singer Mick Jackson (no relation), peaked at No. 61 on the *Billboard* Hot 100. ABOVE RIGHT International versions of the "Blame It On The Boogie" single were released with different picture covers. OPPOSITE The brothers showcased their dance moves for the video of "Blame It On The Boogie."

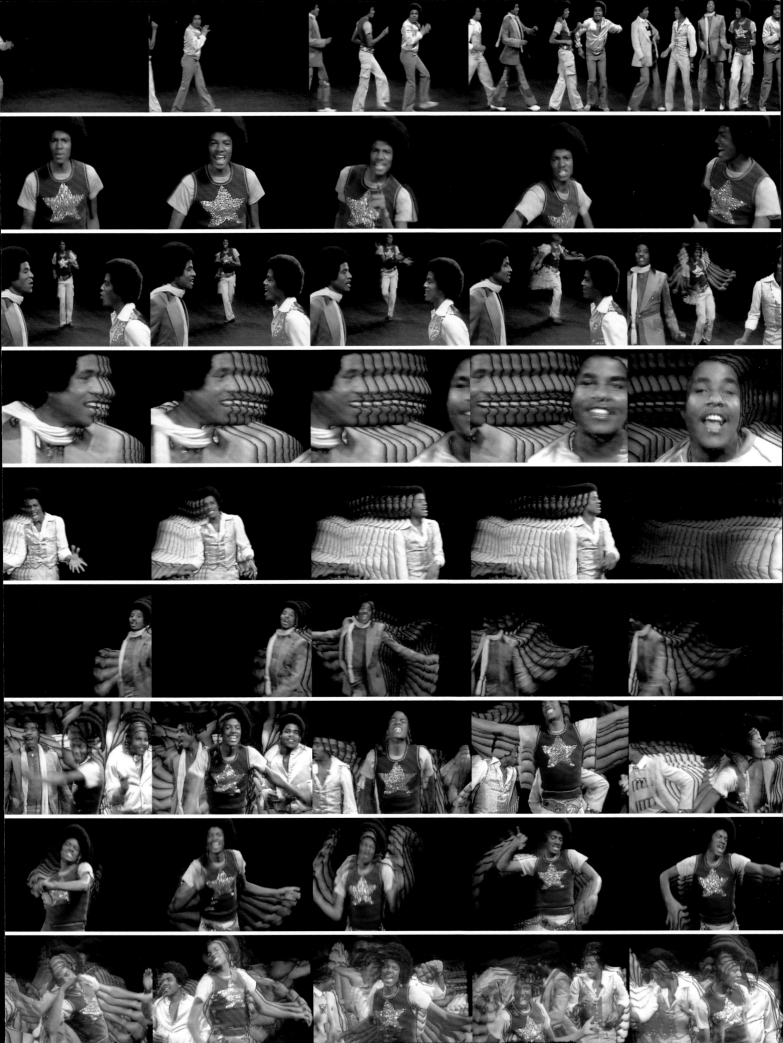

OPPOSITE AND ABOVE The *Destiny* tour began on January 22, 1979, in Bremen, Germany, and ended on September 26, 1980, at the Forum in Inglewood, California.

ABOVE Between 1972 and 1975, Motown released four solo Michael Jackson albums and a greatest hits collection. When the Jacksons signed with Epic as a group, Michael also signed to the label as a solo artist. His first album for Epic on his own was *Off The Wall*, produced by Quincy Jones. The singles "Don't Stop 'Til You Get Enough" and "Rock With You" both went to No. 1 on the *Billboard* Hot 100; the title track and "She's Out Of My Life" both peaked at No. 10. **OPPOSITE** Michael in the spotlight, the place where he was most comfortable.

ABOVE *Triumph* was the fourth Jacksons album to be released on Epic and the first to make the Top 10 of the *Billboard* album chart, peaking at No. 10. The first single, "Lovely One," was the highest-ranking of the album's four charted entries, reaching No. 12. When *Triumph* went to No. 1 on the *Billboard* R&B album chart on November 8, 1980, it was the first Jacksons album to achieve pole position since *Maybe Tomorrow* in 1971. **OPPOSITE** The brothers performed choreography by Michael, Jackie, and Marlon on the highly acclaimed *Triumph* tour.

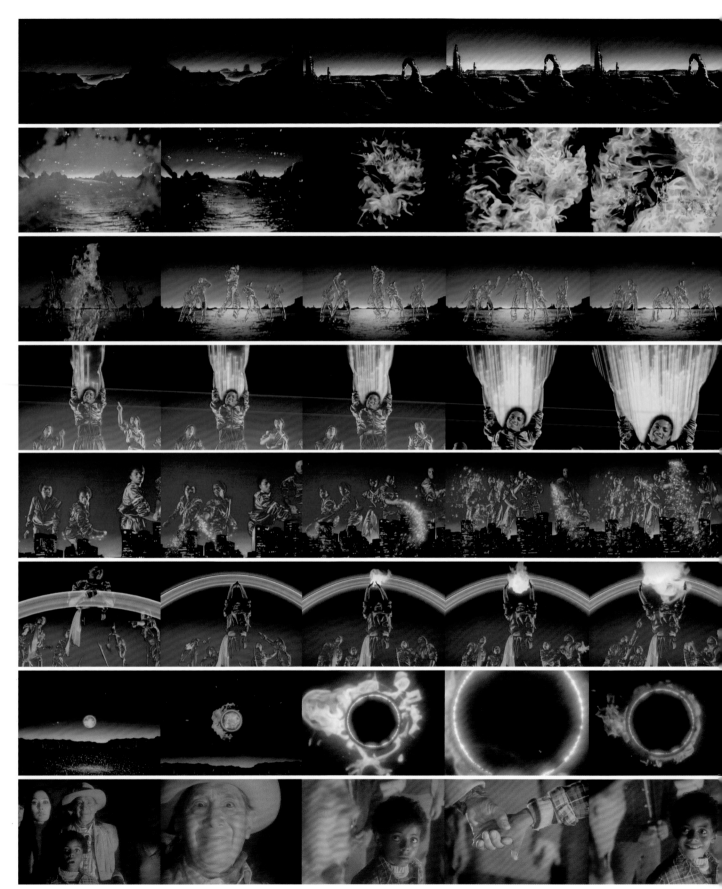

ABOVE Michael came up with the concept for the music video to "Can You Feel It." Bruce Gowers and Robert Abel directed the piece, and Abel's company provided the special effects. Two of Tito's sons—Taj and Taryll—had roles as extras in the video.

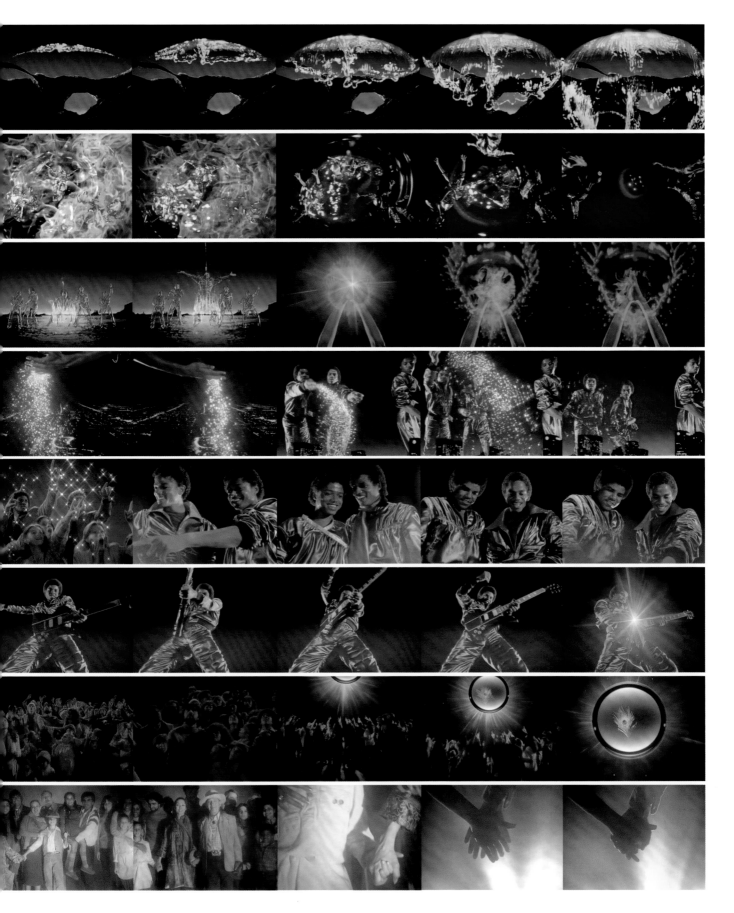

OPPOSITE Accompanied by Michael, Jackie, and Randy, Tito wore a cowboy hat backstage at Reunion Arena in Dallas on July 11, 1981, on the *Triumph* tour. **ABOVE** The cowboy hat was just one of many different hats that Tito wore during his years on stage. "I've always been a hat guy," he told the *New York Post*, "but as I got older, I started to spend a lot more time in the UK. I adopted the bowler hat, and every time I went there I bought more. It became my signature. My brothers used to tell me not to wear [it] because it makes me look older. But it's my head and I like it."

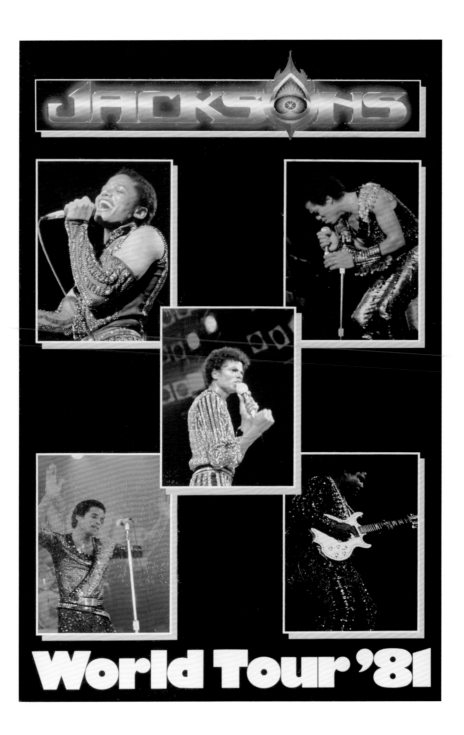

ABOVE In 1981, the Jacksons embarked on the *Triumph* tour of North America, beginning on July 8 in Memphis, Tennessee, and finishing at the Forum, Inglewood, California, on September 26.

ABOVE Since the live album recorded in Japan in 1973 wasn't available in the USA until 2004, *The Jacksons: Live*—released on November 28, 1981—was the group's first live album issued in North America. Recorded during the *Triumph* tour, it opened with "Can You Feel It" and included a medley of "I Want You Back," "ABC," and "The Love You Save."

OPPOSITE This scene is from the music video to "Billie Jean," the second single from *Thriller*. The song topped the *Billboard* Hot 100 for seven weeks, thus becoming Michael's longest-running No. 1 at the time. **ABOVE** With *Thriller* achieving a thirty-seven-week reign at the top of the US charts, Michael Jackson holds the record for the most weeks at No. 1 as an individual artist. The album is certified thirty-three times platinum in the USA and has sold 65 million copies worldwide, making it the biggest-selling album of all time.

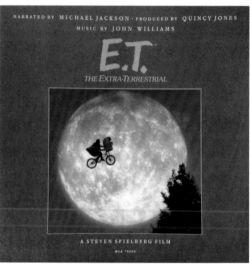

PREVIOUS Michael asked John Landis, director of *An American Werewolf in London*, to direct the video for "Thriller." The result: a fourteen-minute "horror film" that had its world premiere on MTV on December 2, 1983. With makeup by creature designer Rick Baker and choreography by Michael Peters, who won a Tony Award for *Dreamgirls* on Broadway, the video for "Thriller" won a Grammy and was the first music video inducted into the National Film Registry by the US Library of Congress. As of May 2017, "Thriller" has had more than **412 million** views on YouTube. **ABOVE** Michael loved the movie *E.T. the Extra-Terrestrial* so much that he wanted to work with Steven Spielberg on the audiobook and was asked to narrate the story of the lovable alien who comes to Earth but wants to return home. The photograph of Michael with E.T. that graced the cover of *Ebony* in December 1982 was included with the album as a poster.

ABOVE In 1983, the Jacksons World Club issued a kit that was sent
to all official members of the fan club in the USA. The kit contained
photographs, biographies, and a special fan club 45 rpm record,
as well as a newsletter, membership card, and poster.

MICHAEL JACKSON, IN *MOONWALK*:

"SUCCESS DEFINITELY BRINGS ON LONELINESS. PEOPLE THINK YOU'RE LUCKY, THAT YOU HAVE EVERYTHING. THEY THINK YOU CAN GO ANYWHERE AND DO ANYTHING, BUT THAT'S NOT THE POINT. ONE HUNGERS FOR THE BASIC STUFF."

OPPOSITE The brothers played on the Jacksons softball team at Balboa Park, near their home in Encino. There were thirty-five teams in the Showbiz Softball League, with more than 700 players. Games were held on Saturdays, with celebrities such as Tony Danza, Mark Harmon, and Kevin Dobson competing. The park's recreational director, Jim Duran, told the *Los Angeles Times* that although Michael didn't play on the team, he would occasionally show up for games and stand on the sidelines wearing a disguise. "But I can recognize him and people crowd around him."

YESTERDAY

TODAY

FOREVER

ABOVE The classic roster of Motown artists gathered at Pasadena Civic Auditorium in Southern California on March 25, 1983, to record a television special celebrating the twenty-fifth anniversary of the legendary label. **OPPOSITE** Randy and Jermaine joined Michael, Marlon, Tito, and Jackie on stage for a medley of Jackson 5 hits. Then Michael performed the only non-Motown song included in the broadcast: "Billie Jean." His moonwalk was an unforgettable moment of television history, a star turn that put his *Thriller* album on course to become the best-selling album of all time.

ABOVE AND OPPOSITE On November 30, 1983, the Jacksons held a press conference at New York's Tavern on the Green in Central Park to announce the *Victory* tour. All six brothers wore sunglasses during the event, which included a speech by promoter Don King. **OVERLEAF** Janet Jackson worked with her brothers in the studio in 1984 on her second album for the A&M label, *Dream Street*. Marlon produced the initial single, "Don't Stand Another Chance," and sang backing vocals along with Jackie, Tito, Jermaine, and Michael. The song peaked at No. 9 on *Billboard*'s Hot Black Singles chart.

ABOVE This Pepsi commercial was filmed in 1984. Twelve-year-old Alfonso Ribeiro, who later starred in *The Fresh Prince of Bel-Air*, played a Michael Jackson fan who moonwalks into his idol and ends up dancing with him. Ribeiro still owns the red jacket he wore in the video.

PEPSI

PEPSI
THE CHOICE OF
A NEW GENERATION

VICTORY & BEYOND.

JERMAINE LEAVES MOTOWN AND SIGNS WITH ARISTA RECORDS. ALL SIX BROTHERS
GO OUT ON THE ROAD TOGETHER ON THE MASSIVE ALL-STADIUM *VICTORY* TOUR, PLAYING FIFTY-FIVE SHOWS
IN TWENTY-ONE CITIES ACROSS NORTH AMERICA. MICHAEL MAKES CHART HISTORY WITH FIVE NO. 1
SINGLES FROM ONE ALBUM, *BAD*. MARLON AND JACKIE RELEASE SOLO ALBUMS.
THE JACKSON 5 IS INDUCTED INTO THE ROCK AND ROLL HALL OF FAME.

QUINCY JONES WAS a talented young arranger, who was working with well-known artists such as Dinah Washington, Ray Charles, and Sarah Vaughan when he was hired to join the A&R staff at Chicago-based Mercury Records. He signed a teenager from Tenafly, New Jersey, to the label and, as her producer, scored his first No. 1 single on the *Billboard* Hot 100 when Lesley Gore's "It's My Party" assumed pole position the week of June 1, 1963.

Quincy had to wait sixteen-and-a-half years for his next chart-topper, "Don't Stop 'Til You Get Enough," Michael Jackson's first No. 1 on Epic.

Michael Jackson was only twelve years old when he met Quincy Jones. They didn't become close friends until they worked together on the motion-picture adaptation of the Broadway musical *The Wiz* in 1978. Michael was cast as the Scarecrow and Quincy produced the soundtrack. "After *The Wiz* I called him and said, 'Look, I'm going to do an album. Do you think you could recommend some producers?'" Michael wrote in *Moonwalk*. "I wasn't hinting. My question was a naïve but honest one. We talked about music for a while, and, after coming up with some names and some half-hearted hemming and hawing, he said, 'Why don't you let me do it?' I really hadn't thought of it. It sounded to him as if I was hinting, but I wasn't. I just didn't think he would be that interested in my music."

Their collaboration on *Off The Wall* was an incredible success, which resulted in worldwide sales of 20 million copies. No wonder Quincy also produced the follow-up, *Thriller*. While they were making the album, Michael let it be known that his goal was to produce the biggest-selling album of all time. He succeeded. After his duet with Paul McCartney on "The Girl Is Mine" peaked at No. 2, the next two singles—"Billie Jean" and "Beat It"—both went to No. 1 and the following four singles—"Wanna Be Startin' Somethin," "Human Nature," "P. Y. T. (Pretty Young Thing)," and "Thriller"—all reached the Top 10, thus giving Michael seven Top 10 songs from one album, a record at the time.

Michael worked with Quincy one more time, on the *Bad* album, and again set a chart record when the first five singles—"I Just Can't Stop Loving You," "Bad," "The Way You Make Me Feel," "Man In The Mirror," and "Dirty Diana"—all went to No. 1.

While Michael continued his solo work with albums such as *Dangerous*; *HIStory: Past, Present And Future, Book I* and *Invincible*, his brothers were forging ahead with their own solo careers.

Jermaine Jackson continued to record solo works for Motown and released his ninth set for the label, *Let Me Tickle Your Fancy*. Joe Jackson then told his son that he had gone as far as he could go at Motown and that he should meet with Clive Davis. "Before I went to see Clive...I needed to speak with Mr. Gordy," Jermaine wrote in *You Are Not Alone: Michael, Through a Brother's Eyes*. "I couldn't...jump ship without letting him know. When we had the 'big talk,' we both knew that my solo career and producer work had exhausted all their options at Motown and that our professional relationship had reached a natural end. But that didn't make my heart weigh any lighter. As we talked, he made it easier for me. 'You and Hazel need to see how it is to work with other people,' he told me, 'and get out from under my wings. As your father-in-law, I want to see you grow.' Although several years remained on my contract, he released me, and after fourteen years at Motown I left with immense gratitude, with songs still inside me."

A meeting at Clive's private bungalow at the Beverly Hills Hotel resulted in Jermaine signing with Arista Records. His first album for the label, simply titled *Jermaine Jackson*, included two Top 20 singles. Jermaine was hoping that a new duet with his brother Michael would be a huge hit, but Michael's label wouldn't allow a single release for "Tell Me I'm Not Dreamin'." Despite not being released as a single, the track received an enormous amount of radio airplay. Jermaine recorded two more albums for Arista before moving over to LaFace Records for one more release. In 2012, he issued another solo work, *I Wish You L.O.V.E.*

Marlon Jackson recorded his first solo album in 1987. *Baby Tonight* was issued on Capitol Records.

MARLON JACKSON: The Jacksons were sitting dormant at Epic Records, not doing anything, and I decided to do my own album. Walter Yetnikoff let me off to record solo. I really enjoyed doing that record. The single "Don't Go" was No. 2 on the R&B charts, so people embraced it. And then I did a second

album that was never released. It was a pretty good album and there are some songs on there that may get issued one day. There is one song on the album that I'd like to use somewhere else. It was called "Mandela Cry," which I wrote about Nelson Mandela.

After recording a solo album for Motown in 1973, Jackie Jackson released *Be The One* in 1989 on the Polydor label. The last member of the original Jackson 5 to record a solo album was Tito, whose *Tito Time* was released in 2016.

It wasn't only the male members of the Jackson family who recorded solo works and charted in *Billboard*. Rebbie, LaToya, and, of course, Janet were also successful with their own singles and albums, making the Jackson family the only collection of nine brothers and sisters to all appear on the charts as individuals.

After *Destiny* in 1978, the Jacksons released three more albums on Epic: *Triumph* in 1980, *Victory* in 1984, and *2300 Jackson Street* in 1989.

Four singles were released from *Triumph*: "Lovely One," "Heartbreak Hotel," "Can You Feel It," and "Walk Right Now."

TITO JACKSON: "Lovely One" was written by Michael and Randy. Musically, I like it very much. When you write these songs, you don't realize at that moment the impact they're going to have on people. Ever since we wrote it, people use the phrase "lovely one" a lot. "Heartbreak Hotel" is very creative and we put a lot of sound effects into that song. Back then, they didn't have samples so we had to bring people in to create the sound of falling down stairs or whatever effect we wanted. Recording that song was like making a movie with all of the effects. Later on, the title was changed to "This Place Hotel" but I don't know why. Elvis had a song with the same title, but other people have recorded songs with the title "Heartbreak Hotel," too.

The follow-up to "Heartbreak Hotel" was "Can You Feel It," a song written by Jackie and Michael.

JACKIE JACKSON: I was dating Kathy Hilton, Paris's mom, for two or three years. One morning, I was leaving Kathy's house at the top of Mulholland Drive,

and the whole idea for the song came into my mind like an anthem. I was driving along Mulholland and I kept singing the melody, with the drums and music and everything. I had a little Dictaphone in the car and I put everything on that phone. I got to the house in Encino and went right to the piano. Michael said, "What's that? I like it. Can I write that with you?" I said, "Sure." And that's how we wrote "Can You Feel It." When the song came out, it was a sleeper. It didn't start making noise until maybe fifteen years later. We still do it live; it's a song we often open up with. And you know, if I hadn't had that Dictaphone in the car, I wouldn't have remembered some parts of the song by the time I got home. The first time you come up with a song, it's like magic. Sometimes you can't get that back, which is why you've got to record it right away. You try to remember, but it's never quite like it was at first.

The first single issued from *Victory* was "State Of Shock," which featured vocals by the front man for the Rolling Stones.

JACKIE: We weren't in the studio at the time when they did that, just Michael. But the finished product sounded incredible and it captured Mick [Jagger] really well. Michael told me that when Mick was in the studio he was worried that he wasn't going to deliver like Michael wanted him to. Michael had to reassure him, "No man, you're doing a great job. Keep doing what you're doing." Because Mick wanted to impress all of us.

"State Of Shock" peaked at No. 3 on the *Billboard* Hot 100, which made it the Jacksons' biggest hit since "Dancing Machine" went to No. 2 ten years earlier. The follow-up was "Torture," cowritten by Jackie and Kathy Wakefield.

KATHY WAKEFIELD: The Jacksons and I were friends from Motown, when Michael had to stand on a box to reach the mic. They recorded two or three songs of mine as the Jackson 5. After Motown, Jermaine and I worked together on songs for him and others. Jackie and I also stayed in touch. [One day] Jackie called and said he had a track ready for me to work on, already titled "Torture." He laughed later, when I took the lyric in the direction I did—but it worked out well and everyone loved it, including Michael when he came to the session to add his vocal.

Victory wasn't only the name of an album. It was also the name of one of the most successful tours of all time.

MARLON: The whole [*Victory*] tour was stadiums, except for Madison Square Garden. I'm not sure why we appeared there because we also did Giants Stadium [in East Rutherford, New Jersey]. It was an exciting tour. Everything was going right. After *Motown 25* and Michael's incredible solo success, there was a hunger to see us. We rehearsed for quite a while, but I wasn't worried about how long it took; everything had to be right because it was one of our biggest moments. It was a huge undertaking. They had to build an extra large stage because it was an all-stadium tour. That meant more of everything— more lighting, more sound. We had a huge entourage, too, and we went to Kansas City a week before the opening night there so we could rehearse even more, with all the moving parts. It was a big, expensive production.

In his book *Moonwalk*, Michael admitted that he didn't want to do the *Victory* tour, but agreed to be part of it because his brothers wanted to do it. "My goal for the *Victory* tour was to give each performance everything I could. I hoped people might come to see me who didn't even like me. I hoped they might hear about the show and want to see what's going on." Michael explained why the tour made him feel so powerful. "I felt on top of the world. I felt determined.... At the beginning of the show, we rose out of the stage and came down these stairs. The opening was dramatic and bright, and captured the whole feeling of the show. When the lights came on and [the audience] saw us, the roof would come off the place."

Not everything went smoothly. On the last day of rehearsal, Jackie had to have knee surgery.

JACKIE: I had arthroscopic surgery. I went on the road on crutches and I would come on to the stage only here and there. So I wasn't really part of the whole *Victory* tour like my brothers, but I was there with them all the time, sometimes singing on the side of the stage. There was a lot of pain at first and I had a therapist with me on the road. I had to exercise a lot as part of my recovery.

TITO: One of our dreams was to do stadiums like the Beatles, and with the *Victory* tour we got there. We broke a lot of records in the cities that we visited. We were doing three stadium shows in some cities, selling out all three nights. In Los Angeles, we performed six nights at Dodger Stadium, all sold out. It was definitely the biggest tour we'd ever done, with twenty semi-diesel tractors and a crew of 400 people. It took a day-and-a-half to set up the two stages. We used a lot of theatrics in the show, things people had never seen or done before.

One thing the *Victory* tour didn't have was an encore.

TITO: When the audience knows it's your last song, about a quarter of them are already out the door, because they want to get out of the parking lot before it's jammed. So we can't run out the backstage door and head back to our hotel because the roads are already full. You try to leave people much more excited than they were when they walked in the door, and leave them remembering and wanting to hear more.

After fifty-five shows in a row, played in twenty-one cities across the USA and Canada, the *Victory* tour came to an end in December 1984 with the six-night stand at Dodger Stadium in Los Angeles.

TITO: I wanted to continue the tour for as long as we could, but the brothers wanted to take a break. I thought we could have taken thirty days off, rested, and picked it right back up. It should have been for the world to see.

Seven weeks after the final date of the *Victory* tour, six of the Jacksons were back in the recording studio, but they weren't working on a Jacksons album. Michael, Marlon, Jackie, Tito, Randy, and LaToya assembled at A&M Studios in Hollywood just after 10 p.m., following the live broadcast of the twelfth annual American Music Awards. They were there with a large array of superstars, including Diana Ross, Bruce Springsteen, Ray Charles, Kenny Loggins, Bette Midler, Willie Nelson, Cyndi Lauper, Smokey Robinson, Dionne Warwick, and more than a couple of dozen others. They were there to record a song written by Lionel Richie and Michael Jackson, "We Are The World."

JACKIE: Michael called and asked Marlon, Tito, Jermaine, and me to come down to A&M, which was on the site of the former Charlie Chaplin Studios. He said, "Just come down," but he didn't tell us why. We saw him in the studio and he said, "We're going to do a song." And they played it over and over on the speakers. Everybody else got a copy ahead of time, but not us. Michael knew we would catch on quickly. We know his style, right? So they kept playing, "We are the world, we are the children." It was easy. To see everybody there under one roof was amazing.

TITO: Quincy Jones told everybody, "This is not for us. This is not our single. This is a single for the world. It's for Africa mainly, so we're not going to trip on who's singing the best." He told us all to leave our egos at the door. But it was a lot of fun, seeing all the celebrities, friends, and colleagues. I hadn't seen Lionel Richie in a while. The Jackson 5 and the Commodores were really good friends for a time. We did a couple tours together, so we would hang out in our hotel rooms and write music and just be kids. They were older than us but not that much older.

Richie spoke to *Billboard* and admitted, "I can't really say how the song came about. Neither one of us saw the other put his hands on the keyboard. That's how we write. He brought in an idea, I brought in an idea; we went back, we listened, and then we smashed both ideas together. The music came first. As for the lyrics...they just kind of flowed.... I'd throw out a line, Michael would come back with a greater line—the same one, with the words changed around differently—and I'd change his line and finally we'd have this wonderful line."

JACKIE: When it was over, everybody was giving autographs to everyone else and trading phone numbers. We were just singing background vocals, so we were only there for about two hours. LaToya was there, too, and later we found out that Janet was upset because no one had called her. She was so mad; she was crying. No one asked Janet to join the party.

At 3:50 p.m. Greenwich Mean Time on April 5, 1985, some 5,000 radio stations around the world played the song that had been recorded to raise money to help feed the starving people of Africa and the USA. One week later, the song began a four-week run at No. 1 on the *Billboard* Hot 100. It was the fifth chart-topper written by Michael, following three of his own solo hits and a duet with Paul McCartney ("Say, Say, Say").

Marlon remained involved with USA for Africa long after the recording session.

MARLON: I was invited to go with them to Ethiopia, and from that point forward I sat on the Board of Directors. Producing the song was only one part. Next we had to make sure that the money got to where it needed to be. That was one thing we were very conscious of. We made sure that if Ethiopia needed more trucks, we would buy the trucks and be certain they would arrive and be used for the right purpose. We chartered a 747 cargo plane from the Flying Tiger Line, which is now FedEx. We sat upstairs, and downstairs was full of medicine, food, and things that were needed. I was in Ethiopia for two weeks, with organizers Harry Belafonte and Ken Kragen and two doctors. It was amazing.

After *Victory*, the Jacksons waited five years before they released their next album. *2300 Jackson Street*, named for their home address in Gary, Indiana, is the group's final album to date. There are only four Jacksons pictured on the cover: Jermaine, Randy, Jackie, and Tito. Michael and Marlon were both out of the group but made guest appearances on the album.

TITO: After the *Victory* album, we wanted to do another record. At that time, our label wasn't really involved. They didn't say, "Go into the studio and record an album. Here's the budget." So we started making [*2300 Jackson Street*] on our own, and eventually Sony [parent company of Epic] supported the recording. But we tried to make the album different. We worked with a few different people, and also tried to make a different sound. We had producers like Michael Omartian. I sang lead with Jermaine on one song, "Art Of Madness," written by Omartian and Bruce Sudano with Jermaine.

Kenny "Babyface" Edmonds and L. A. Reid produced the album's first single, "Nothin' (That Compares 2 U)." The title track, which was the second single released from the album, featured other members of the Jackson family, including sisters Rebbie and Janet.

JACKIE: The idea came from Teddy Riley, but the melodies came from us. Teddy came up with the title track and we all wrote it. It's a beautiful song, and we included vocals by some of our nieces and nephews on the track. You can hear the voices of Jermaine's kids and some of the other brothers' kids. It was a headache trying to get them together because they were all talking and we had to keep saying, "Quiet! Quiet!" But it was fun and we really enjoyed it, even though it's hard working with kids in the studio because they don't know any better. At the time, my son was five years old and it was still difficult.

TITO: The idea of the album was to sum up and talk about our roots, where we came from, and to thank our parents for what they have done.

The final track on *2300 Jackson Street* enjoyed exposure beyond the album's popularity in 1989. When the brothers organized *The Jackson Family Honors* television special, broadcast on NBC in 1994, "If You'd Only Believe" was chosen as the theme song. Jermaine, the main force behind the evening, said that the show was designed to honor humanitarians. Among those receiving awards were Elizabeth Taylor and Berry Gordy.

"If You'd Only Believe" was written by Jermaine, with songwriters Roxanne Seeman and Billie Hughes.

ROXANNE SEEMAN: Jermaine has always had the utmost respect for the work of a lyricist. Sometimes he would ask me what I meant by a line or lines I had written, not because it wasn't understandable but because he wanted to get the inspiration and meaning of the words into his interpretation of the lyrics when he sang them. The verse lyrics for "If You'd Only Believe" were inspired by Victor Hugo's *Les Misérables* and [the character] Jean Valjean: "I have seen love make men stagger, Prey on their weakness and wound their pride, But you won't be touched by its dagger, When you're close by my side." Jermaine called and said he wanted to record "If You'd Only Believe" and was making an album with his brothers and Michael

Omartian. They recorded "If You'd Only Believe" at Tito's. He had a beautiful studio in his home, on top of a hillside in Encino, and we were invited there.

The Jackson Family Honors was not the only television project that the brothers were involved with during the post-*Victory* years. In 1992, Suzanne de Passe and Jermaine were two of the producers on the miniseries *The Jacksons: An American Dream*. Lawrence Hilton-Jacobs and Angela Bassett portrayed Joseph and Katherine Jackson in the four-hour production, broadcast in the USA on ABC.

JACKIE: Before production started, I met Terrence Howard. I knew his work in films and he told me, "Jackie, I'm playing you." I said, "Well, do a good job. Make me look good." We had lunch and hung out. He asked me about touring and how we got started. He did a wonderful job; I was really impressed. But the miniseries portrayed my dad as the meanest guy in the world. He was hard, but not like that. They needed some drama.

TITO: I wasn't involved very much, but it was a pretty good portrayal of my family. They dramatized certain situations to make it more interesting, but they touched on everything. I spent time with the actor who played me, Angel Vargas. I was living in the Channel Islands at the time, and he came out to the house and spent a couple of days with me. It was strange, because he was watching me, trying to figure out my gestures. Then he started imitating me. He did a very good job but when you watch someone playing you, it's not quite you.

In 1995, the next generation of Jacksons made an impact on the *Billboard* charts.

TITO: My three boys came home one day after seeing a Jacksons show, and they grabbed mops and put on a Jackson 5 record and began mimicking the brothers. They said, "We want to be like our uncles." I gave them instruments and they rehearsed. I wasn't going to push this on them. If they liked it I would support them, but they had to really want it because I knew the business was not easy. My engineer and I worked with them, and they recorded some demos. They called themselves 3T, and Michael said, "You

guys should be with Sony. No one sells more records than Epic." Their single "Anything" reached the Top 15 on the *Billboard* charts.

"Anything" wasn't just a domestic hit in the USA. The single entered the Top 10 in Australia, France, Ireland, Norway, New Zealand, the Netherlands, Sweden, and the UK.

It's not hard to figure out how 3T chose their name, once you know the names of Tito's three sons: Toriano Adaryll Jackson, Jr. (a.k.a. Taj), Taryll Adren Jackson, and Tito Joe Jackson (a.k.a. T.J.).

TITO: My middle son took a few little guitar lessons, but my youngest kid is more interested in the guitar today. I remember when I used to put him on my lap and hold the guitar. He would cry and didn't want to have anything to do with it. Recently, he told me, "Dad, remember when you used to put me in your lap and make me play the guitar and I would cry? I didn't want to do it and I would squirm out. I'm so mad at myself today, because I love the guitar and I wish I had learned it." I told him, "I couldn't make you do it." My sons still play music and they've performed in England and Holland. I give them advice but they don't take it. They're my kids, what am I going to do?!

The Jacksons made another television appearance when the twelfth annual Rock and Roll Hall of Fame Induction was broadcast on VH1 on May 8, 1997. The ceremony was held three nights earlier in Cleveland, where the Jackson 5 was inducted by Diana Ross.

TITO: To be inducted into the Rock and Roll Hall of Fame made me feel that I had made it. It's like getting your certificate or your diploma. You're in the club now. You did it, welcome aboard. We were inducted along with the Bee Gees, and that was exciting because they were one of the groups we idolized. We followed them when we were amateurs and they were a brother family act. We had a lot in common, so it was great to be inducted with the Bee Gees.

All six Jackson brothers were together again in New York City on September 7, 2001, for a thirtieth anniversary celebration of Michael's solo career, which began in

1971 with the release of the single "Got To Be There." The two-night concert, which also filled the venue on September 10, was edited into a television special that aired on CBS in November 2001. The roster of stars performing Michael Jackson songs included James Ingram and Gloria Estefan ("I Just Can't Stop Loving You"), Billy Gilman ("Ben"), Usher, Mya, and Whitney Houston ("Wanna Be Startin' Somethin'"), Marc Anthony ("She's Out Of My Life"), and Liza Minnelli ("You Are Not Alone").

The Jacksons also appeared on the bill, turning to songs such as "I Want You Back," "ABC," "The Love You Save," "I'll Be There," "Can You Feel It," and "Shake Your Body (Down To The Ground)," and they were joined on stage by *NSYNC for "Dancing Machine." Michael's solo performances included "Billie Jean" and "You Rock My World;" he also performed "The Way You Make Me Feel" with Britney Spears and "Black Or White" with Slash.

The musical director for the two shows was Greg Phillinganes, who had filled the same role on Michael's solo tours and had been involved with all of his solo albums.

GREG PHILLINGANES: It was without question one of the highest moments in my entire career to MD and celebrate the anniversary of all of the Jackson brothers. When I consider my journey with them— beginning as a captivated fan in junior high school all the way to backstage at Madison Square Garden—explaining to them how special it was for me [to be MD] and to tell them "Have a great show" was totally surreal.

The morning after the second show was also surreal for all those involved. They woke up in their Manhattan hotels to a terrorist attack on the USA. There were thirty-two members of the Jackson family in New York City at the time. "I saw the plane coming down," says Jackie of the first airplane that crashed into the World Trade Center. "My son was out visiting some of his friends...and I couldn't find him." Janet Jackson called her friend Colin Powell, who assisted the Jacksons in getting out of the city on a day when all flights in the USA were grounded. The Jacksons boarded a bus and were driven to another group of buses, all lined up in a row. "They took us to LA," Jackie recalls. "That's how we got out."

ABOVE Michael Whelan painted the cover of the *Victory* album. He is best known
for his cover illustrations for novels by science-fiction authors such as Isaac Asimov,
Ray Bradbury, Arthur C. Clarke, and Robert Heinlein, as well as fantasy and horror writer
Stephen King. Michael Jackson selected Whelan for the *Victory* artwork and requested
something similar to the artist's painting on the cover of Asimov's *Foundation's Edge*.
Michael asked Whelan to place him behind his brothers, but also requested for his glove
and socks to glow. **OPPOSITE** This photograph was taken at the session that produced
some of the images that were used on the inside cover of the *Victory* album.

ABOVE This plaque was presented by Epic Records to Jackie to celebrate the gold single for "State Of Shock" and the triple-platinum status of the *Victory* album. Similar plaques were awarded to his brothers.

ABOVE AND OPPOSITE Tito's star-shaped guitar from the *Victory* tour was made by Yamaha. "I had to be careful with it," he laughs, "because of all the points on it. I always had to look out for it on stage because it was so easy to bump into one of my brothers. I had to move it out of their way. I tried to do it with rhythm so no one would notice.... I only played one song with it, the opening number of the show."

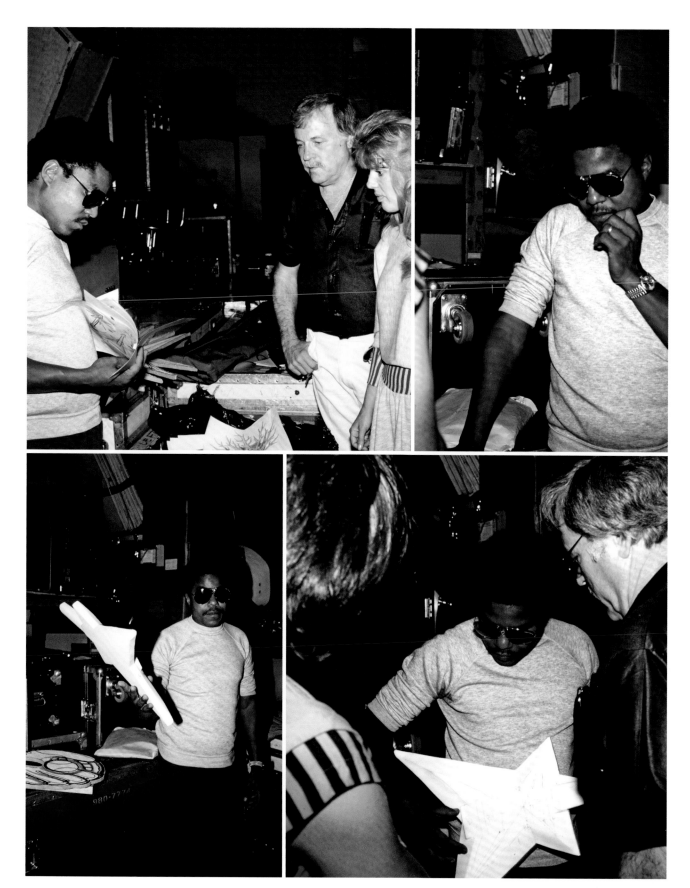

OVERLEAF The music video for "Torture" was directed by Jeff Stein and choreographed by Paula Abdul. The latter's work on the six-minute horror/sci-fi-themed video led to a career in choreographing music videos, including "When I Think Of You," "Nasty," and "What Have You Done For Me Lately?" for Janet Jackson.

ABOVE AND OPPOSITE "I was really into baseball," Tito explains. "...I came up with the idea to have a guitar made with a baseball bat for the neck and a glove for the body.... I still have the guitar. Every once in a while I take it out and play a few chords, but it's awkward—it doesn't feel like a guitar."

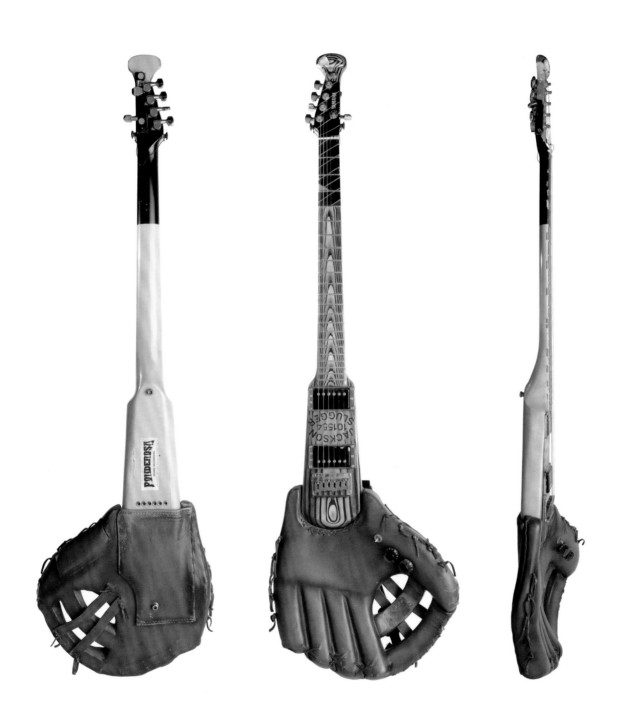

ABOVE The souvenir program for the *Victory* tour was published in 1984. It included photographs of the Jacksons, individually and as a group. **OPPOSITE** A photo session for the *Victory* tour. **OVERLEAF** Pepsi signed up to be a sponsor of the *Victory* tour, despite the fact that Michael did not drink Pepsi. In the terms of the contract, the Jacksons had to film two commercials. The first was shot at the Shrine Auditorium, Los Angeles, in 1984. Michael was dancing on stage when a pyrotechnics display was triggered too early. His hair caught fire and he suffered second-degree burns to his face and scalp.

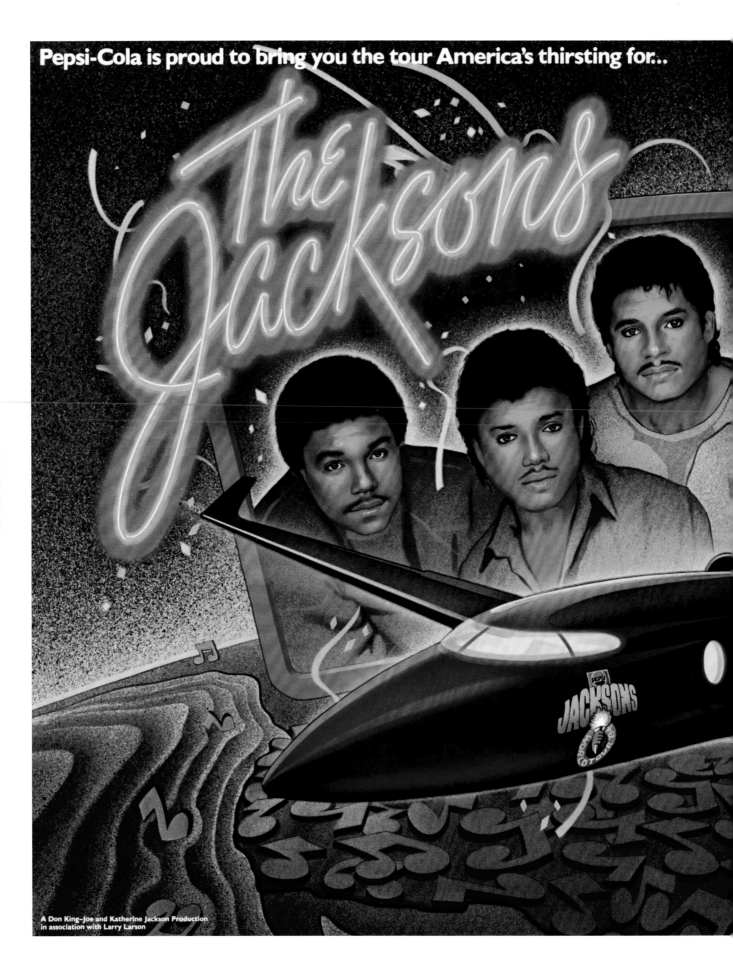

Pepsi-Cola is proud to bring you the tour America's thirsting for...

A Don King–Joe and Katherine Jackson Production
in association with Larry Larson

ABOVE AND OPPOSITE This collection of photographs was taken backstage at the *Victory* tour, the only tour that featured all six Jackson brothers: Jackie, Tito, Jermaine, Marlon, Michael, and Randy.

ABOVE Behind the scenes of the *Victory* tour, which began July 6, 1984, at Arrowhead Stadium in Kansas City and ended on December 9, 1984, at Dodger Stadium in Los Angeles.

ABOVE The Jacksons played a total of fifty-five shows during the *Victory* tour, and performed for more than two million people.

PREVIOUS The Jacksons arrive on stage at the *Victory* tour. Michael described the opening number as "dramatic and bright," as he and his brothers rose up from under the stage and walked down a staircase.

OPPOSITE AND ABOVE Although all six brothers participated on the *Victory* tour, Jackie was sidelined for part of the tour because of a knee injury. He was on crutches for the earlier dates but eventually was able to walk with a cane.

PAGES 232–233 Tito describes how he and his brothers assembled the set list for the *Victory* tour: "We wanted to start with a high-energy song that wasn't one of our No. 1 hits. You want people to be excited when you're hitting the stage. Then you want to keep the energy going for at least three songs. Then you cool the audience down.... You keep the show building and you bring the audience up again for your last two songs and you're out." **PAGES 234–235** The Jacksons filled stadiums every night on the *Victory* tour, often playing three consecutive dates. In Los Angeles, the final city on the tour, they played six nights in a row at Dodger Stadium. **ABOVE AND OPPOSITE** Eight of the fifteen songs on the set list of the *Victory* tour were solo Michael Jackson hits, including "Wanna Be Startin' Somethin'," "Off The Wall," "Rock With You," "Working Day And Night," "Beat It," and "Billie Jean."

JACKIE JACKSON:

"MICHAEL WAS A GENIUS. HE WOULD DANCE EVERY DAY. HE WAS ALWAYS STUDYING THE CRAFT. HE WAS A TALENTED WRITER WHO CREATED GREAT MELODIES. SOME PEOPLE JUST HAVE IT AND HE WAS ONE OF THOSE WHO HAD IT."

OPPOSITE AND OVERLEAF The fedora, the moonwalk, and the single glove were all trademarks of Michael Jackson's massive hit "Billie Jean," the penultimate song performed on stage during the *Victory* tour.

ABOVE AND OPPOSITE In addition to their parents Joe and Katherine, and siblings LaToya and Janet, the Jacksons had many backstage visitors during the *Victory* tour, including Mr. T (top left with eight next-generation Jacksons, including Rebbie's daughter, Marlon's two daughters and a son, Tito's three sons, and Jackie's son), Quincy Jones, Yoko Ono and Sean Lennon, Jim Henson and Kermit the Frog, Danny DeVito, promoter Don King, Tommy Hearns, Donny Osmond, Madonna, and Bill Murray.

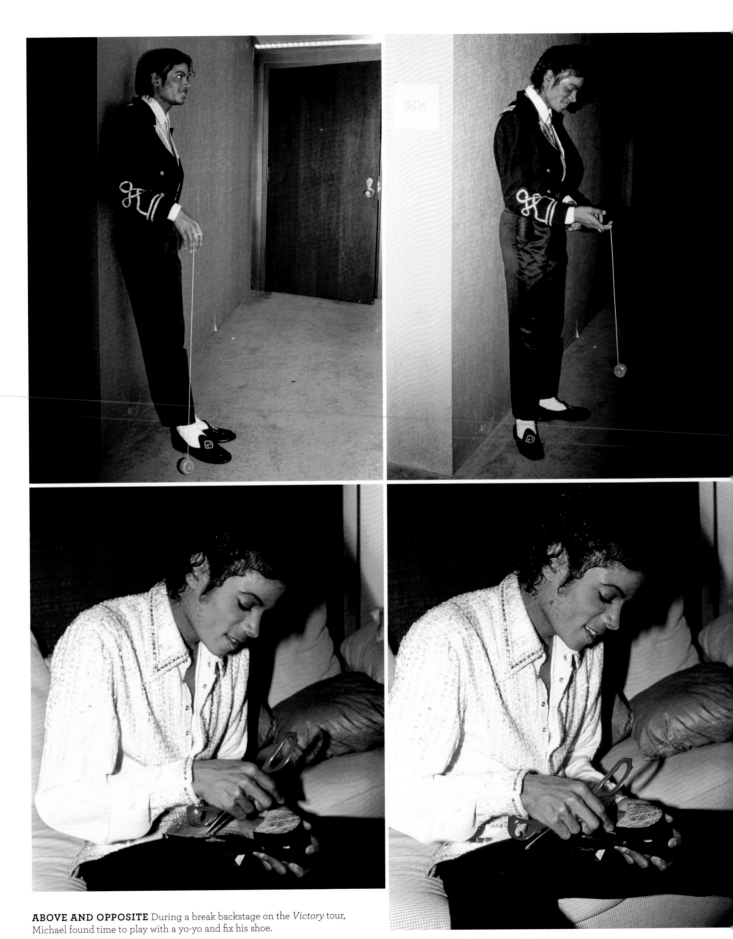

ABOVE AND OPPOSITE During a break backstage on the *Victory* tour, Michael found time to play with a yo-yo and fix his shoe.

ABOVE TOP The Rev. Jesse Jackson visited the Jacksons during the *Victory* tour. **ABOVE** "Madonna's manager, Freddy DeMann, brought her to see us...in New York," Marlon remembers. "He told us, 'This is my next new artist.'"

ABOVE TOP Basketball legend Magic Johnson was a backstage visitor during the *Victory* tour.
ABOVE Two of the O'Jays—Eddie Levert and Walter Williams—also stopped by.

ABOVE AND OPPOSITE Backstage at the *Victory* tour. It was an
elaborate production and magician Franz Harary (opposite) created
an illusion in which Michael disappeared and reappeared on stage.

ABOVE Two of the many photographs taken by Harrison Funk, the Jacksons' official photographer for the *Victory* tour. After the tour, Funk continued to photograph Michael until his passing in 2009.

ABOVE Michael shares a smile with Andy Warhol. Earlier that year Warhol created his iconic portrait of Michael, which appeared on the cover of *Time*. He had met the group on tour before, at Madison Square Garden in 1981.

PREVIOUS The Jacksons had a fifteen-song set list (including some medleys) on the *Victory* tour, but oddly enough none of the songs were from the *Victory* album. **ABOVE AND OPPOSITE** Michael performed alongside his brothers on the *Victory* tour. "Michael worked in the same business as us, but the seat he sat in was above everybody else's," says Tito, "because he deserved to sit there. He was a phenomenon. He was a miracle entertainer. I haven't seen anyone who comes close. He influenced all of them, from Usher to Justin Timberlake to Bruno Mars."

PREVIOUS Tito (center) wailing on guitar, flanked by Marlon (left) and Michael during the *Victory* tour. **ABOVE AND OPPOSITE** More scenes from the *Victory* tour. One of rock's premiere guitarists, Eddie Van Halen, joined Michael on stage at Texas Stadium on July 14, 1984, for "Beat It." Eddie also played guitar on the recording of the song.

ABOVE The six Jackson brothers pose for an advertisement for Yamaha.
The campaign was called "The Fantasy Becomes Reality."

QUINCY JONES
PRODUCTIONS™

January 23, 1985

My Fellow Artists,

We are so happy that you have consented to contribute your talent for
this worthwhile endeavor, the recording of "We Are The World", written
by Michael Jackson and Lionel Richie. How special is this project?
In all the years that I have worked in this business, I have never
seen anything like this. So many kinds of contributions are being
given for such a life or death result. It is gratifying to be able
to say that the entertainment industry is deeply involved in aiding
the poor of the world. Enclosed is the tape of the song and it is
perfect for this cause.

Distribution of the various solo parts have not been decided as yet.
The solo and ensemble parts will all be decided based on the main ob-
jective in the making of this record so that it has the widest appeal.
I am most impressed and moved by the unanimous spirit of all of you
which has been to accept this project with the pride and spirit of
checking your ego at the door. It is so nice to have an occasion where
we can unite as one. It is this spirit that will make this project a
total success.

Please familiarize yourself with the music and lyrics because we have
lots of work to do on January 28th. Please arrive promptly at 10:00 pm
The cassettes
are numbered and I can't express how important it is not to let this
material out of your hands. Please do not make copies and return this
cassette the night of the 28th. We know how easy it is for a tape to get
into a DJ's hands. This tape was purposely made in a rough demo form to
discourage it being used inappropriately.

Ken Kragen and his organization have been the backbone on this project.
They have worked around the clock to insure that every aspect of this
project is coordinated properly. Should you need any assistance, please
do not hesitate to contact Laurel at Ken Kragen's office (213) 854-4400
or Madeline Randolph at Quincy Jones Productions (213) 934-4508.

January 23, 1985
Page 2

I am honored to be associated with all of you. In my 35 years, every
name on this list has a special place in my heart as a creator and a
human being. This is the 'A-team'. Thank you for giving so much of
yourself. All of us appreciate your sacrifice and we will do everything in our power to make this an unforgettable and golden memory.
In the years to come, when your children ask, "what did mommy and
daddy do for the war against world famine?", you can proudly say this
was your contribution.

This cause is close to all of our hearts and our collected contributions
are united at the core; to help feed the hungry of the world.

Fondly,

Quincy Jones

P.S. I will break my buns to make this the most enjoyable experience
you ever had.

Save the Children®

54 Wilton Road
PO Box 950
Westport, CT 06881 USA
(203) 226-7272

February 8, 1985

Tito Jackson
c/o Joe Jackson
Joe Jackson Productions

Dear Tito:

All of us who work to relieve the desperate plight of
the famine-stricken people of Africa are sincerely
touched and most grateful for your participation in
"USA for Africa." All of you who have contributed the
gift of your talents, that others may have the gift
of life, are evidence of the oneness of people. You
provide the encouragement to agencies such as ours to
work the harder for the purposes we all believe in.

As you so appropriately sang, we are the ones to make
a brighter day. Thank you for your efforts to
brighten the future for so many African children and
their families.

Sincerely,

David L. Guyer
President

Serving child, family and community through self-help

The National Academy Of Recording Arts And Sciences®

IS PROUD TO SALUTE
THE PARTICIPATING ARTISTS
ON THE HISTORIC RECORDING

"WE ARE THE WORLD"

Dan Aykroyd	Harry Belafonte	Lindsey Buckingham
Kim Carnes	Ray Charles	Bob Dylan
Sheila E.	Bob Geldof	Hall & Oates
James Ingram	Jackie Jackson	LaToya Jackson
Marlon Jackson	Michael Jackson	Randy Jackson
Tito Jackson	Al Jarreau	Waylon Jennings
Billy Joel	Cyndi Lauper	Huey Lewis & The News
Kenny Loggins	Bette Midler	Willie Nelson
Jeffrey Osborne	Steve Perry	The Pointer Sisters
Lionel Richie	Smokey Robinson	Kenny Rogers
Diana Ross	Paul Simon	Bruce Springsteen
Tina Turner	Dionne Warwick	Stevie Wonder

PRESENTED
FEBRUARY 25, 1986

NATIONAL PRESIDENT

ABOVE Letters and certificates were sent to the Jacksons in connection with their
charitable work for USA for Africa and the recording of "We Are The World."

USA for AFRICA
United Support of Artists for Africa

Columbia
8503

ABOVE TOP This publicity still from Columbia Records shows where all of the artists were standing in the A&M Studios when they recorded "We Are The World." Their places were assigned before they arrived, according to producer Quincy Jones, so no one could take the time to decide where they wanted to stand. **ABOVE** The single and album covers for "We Are The World." **OVERLEAF** The once-in-a-lifetime collection of artists gathered at A&M Studios in Hollywood to record "We Are The World" on the night of January 28, 1984. Many of the vocalists arrived at the studio directly from that evening's live broadcast of the

"TO BE A PART OF THE JACKSONS, BRINGING SMILES TO PEOPLE WHO ENJOY THE MUSIC, MEANS A LOT. IT MEANS THAT YOU'VE DONE SOMETHING WITH YOUR LIFE, OTHER THAN JUST LIVED A LIFE. AND I STILL HAVE A LOT TO GIVE AS DO MY BROTHERS, BECAUSE THE MUSIC JUST FLOWS THROUGH OUR FAMILY."

OPPOSITE The brothers experimented with different looks during the photo session for the *Victory* tour program book.

OPPOSITE Although Jermaine remained with Motown after his brothers left to sign with Epic, he eventually departed Berry Gordy's label and signed with Clive Davis at Arista Records. These shots are from sessions in the studio and on location during his Arista years. **ABOVE** Jermaine's three albums for Arista were *Jermaine Jackson* (1984), *Precious Moments* (1986), and *Don't Take It Personal* (1989), and he also released one album for the LaFace label, *You Said* (1991). **OVERLEAF** "These are some of my favorite photos," says Marlon, "because we love [the] *Our Gang* [comedies] and this is us dressing up as *Our Gang*."

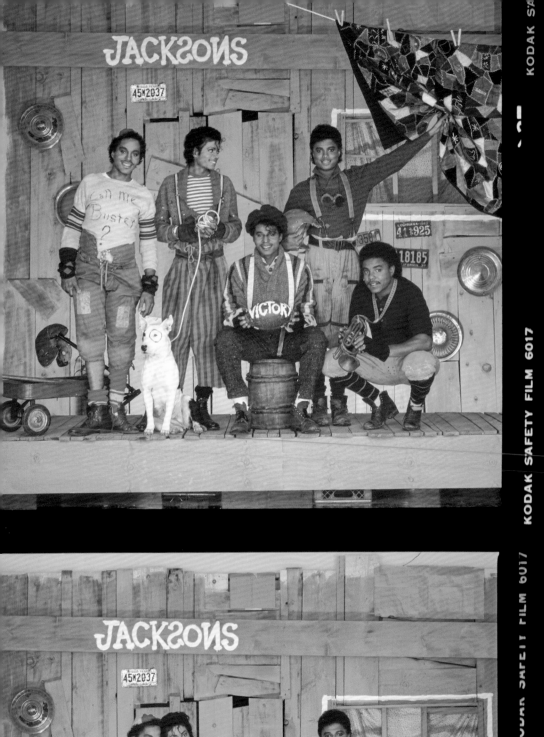

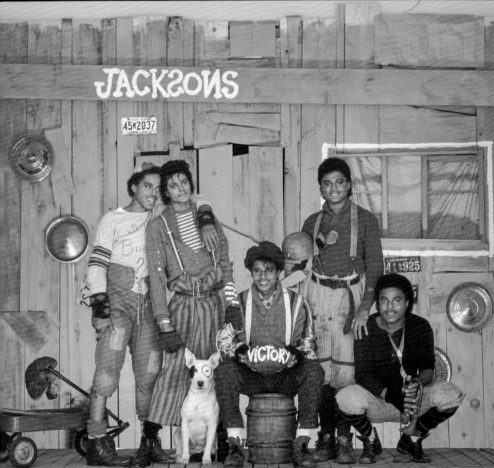

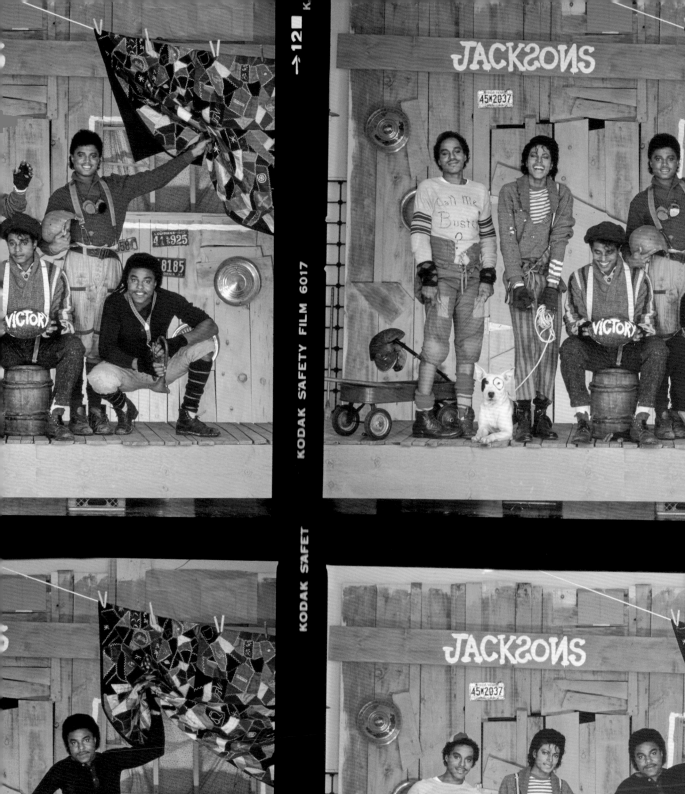

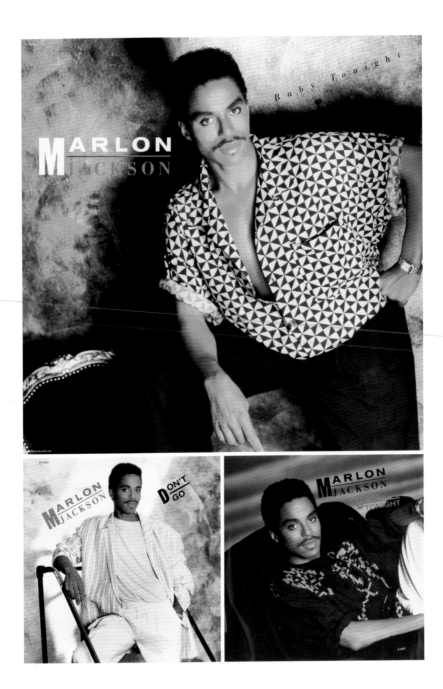

ABOVE TOP "I put a lot of time and energy into my first solo album," says Marlon. I worked with Winston Johnson and Fred Maher from Scritti Politti. Fred was their programmer and we wrote some songs together. We recorded the album in my house in California." **ABOVE** In 1987, "Don't Go" and "Baby Tonight" both appeared on *Billboard*'s Hot Black Singles chart, the former peaking at No. 2 and the latter at No. 57. **OPPOSITE** Recording a solo album also meant doing solo photo sessions, such as this one with Marlon at the water's edge.

PREVIOUS "We went to Malibu one day and took photos with some of our cars," Marlon recalls. "Jackie was standing by my car and I was next to a Porsche and Michael wanted to be by the Knight Rider car." **OPPOSITE** These stills are from Jackie Jackson's solo photo shoots. **ABOVE** Sixteen years after his first solo album, Jackie released a second set on his own, *Be The One*, on the Polydor label. The 1989 CD included the singles "Stay" and "Cruzin." Both appeared on the *Billboard* Hot Black Singles chart.

ABOVE AND OPPOSITE The Jacksons played two nights in Denver in 1984. "We traveled with a photographer," says Tito, "...I told him I wanted to go out and take some photos of the mountains and scenery. I'd never really flown a plane."

MICHAEL JACKSON *Bad*

ABOVE Michael's third solo album for Epic was *Bad*, the follow-up to *Thriller*. Although improving on the sales of *Thriller* was probably an impossible task, *Bad* did carve its own path, making chart history by becoming the first album to yield five No. 1 singles on *Billboard*'s Hot 100. *Bad* did not top the sales of *Thriller*, but it remains one of the best-selling albums of all time, certified ten times platinum in the USA, which represents 10 million copies shipped to stores. **OPPOSITE** The video for "Bad," directed by Martin Scorsese, featured a young Wesley Snipes before he became famous. The video ran eighteen minutes and five seconds and was broadcast in prime time on the CBS television network in the USA.

OPPOSITE These scenes are from the video for the single "2300 Jackson Street," featuring the Jacksons with their siblings Rebbie and Janet, parents Joe and Katherine, and other members of the family. **ABOVE** The front and back covers of the Jacksons' final album for Epic, *2300 Jackson Street*. Released on May 28, 1989, the album featured four Jacksons: Jackie, Tito, Jermaine, and Randy. Michael and Marlon guest-starred on the autobiographical title track.

ABOVE After working with producer Quincy Jones on *Off The Wall*, *Thriller*, and *Bad*, Michael changed things up on his eighth solo album, *Dangerous*. Released on November 26, 1991, it includes tracks produced by Teddy Riley, Bill Bottrell, Bruce Swedien, and Jackson himself. The first single, "Black Or White," was developed from a track written for *Bad*. Michael's twelfth No. 1 as a solo artist, "Black Or White" topped the US singles chart for seven weeks.

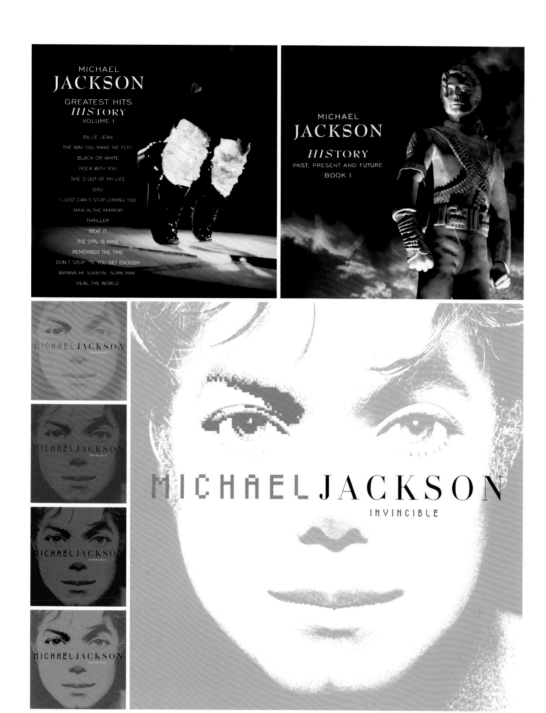

ABOVE On June 18, 1995, Epic released Michael's first double album. *HIStory: Past, Present And Future, Book I* included one disc of greatest hits and one of new material. Preceding the album by three weeks was the first single "Scream," a duet with Janet. It debuted at No. 5 on the *Billboard* Hot 100, the highest entry in that chart's history at the time. The follow-up, "You Are Not Alone," debuted at No. 1 and was the first single ever to do so. In 1997, Michael began work on his next album and continued recording throughout 2001, when it was finally released. *Invincible* debuted at No. 1 on the *Billboard* 200 chart.

ROCK AND ROLL HALL OF FAME® FOUNDATION, INC.

1290 AVENUE OF THE AMERICAS, NEW YORK, NEW YORK 10104
(212) 484-1755
FAX (212) 258-2533

Suzan I. Evans, Esq.
Executive Director

Mr. Marlon Jackson

September 11, 1996

Dear Mr. Jackson:

On behalf of the Rock and Roll Hall of Fame Foundation, it is my pleasure to inform you prior to our official press announcement that you, as a member of Jackson 5, will be inducted into the Hall of Fame at the Twelfth Annual Induction Ceremony on the evening of Thursday, May 15, 1997, at the Rock and Roll Hall of Fame and Museum in Cleveland, Ohio. Kindly contact me in order to discuss further details of your induction and to organize your travel arrangements.

We would like to have your signature inscribed into the glass walls of the Hall of Fame at the Museum. Towards that end, I have enclosed a signature sheet. Please sign your name as you wish it to appear, and fax or mail it to me as soon as possible.

Again, on behalf of the Board, we extend our heartfelt congratulations. We look forward to hearing from you or your representative soon, so that we may begin to plan this significant evening.

Sincerely,

Suzan Evans

Suzan Evans

ABOVE In September 1996, the Jacksons were informed that they were to be inducted into the Rock and Roll Hall of Fame at the twelfth annual ceremony in the Renaissance Hotel in Cleveland, Ohio, in May 1997. **OPPOSITE** After Diana Ross inducted the Jacksons, Motown founder Berry Gordy joined them on stage (above). "They were a cultural revolution," he told the audience. "For the first time, young black kids had their own heroes in their own image to idolize and emulate." Backstage, the Jacksons and Ross met the Bee Gees (below), who were also inducted that day.

ABOVE The brothers hung out in New York City before the "Michael Jackson: 30th Anniversary Celebration." They performed two shows: on September 7 and 10, 2001.

JACKIE JACKSON:

"FOR ME, THE MUSICAL HIGHLIGHT OF OUR ENTIRE CAREER IS 'I WANT YOU BACK'. BECAUSE THAT'S THE ONE THAT PUT THE FLAG IN THE GROUND. WHEN PEOPLE HEAR IT, THEY GO CRAZY. THAT'S THE ONE THAT GOT US KNOWN AROUND THE WORLD AND IT WILL BE WITH US FOR LIFE."

OPPOSITE Scenes from the concert "Michael Jackson: 30th Anniversary Celebration" at Madison Square Garden, New York City.

ABOVE AND OPPOSITE The six Jackson brothers were reunited on stage at Madison Square Garden in New York City on September 7, 2001 (and again on September 10, 2001) for the show "Michael Jackson: 30th Anniversary Celebration." It marked three decades of Michael's solo career, dating back to the release of the single "Got To Be There" in 1971. Segments from the two live concerts were edited into a television special that aired on CBS two months later. Performing "I Want You Back," "Shake Your Body (Down To The Ground)," and other Jackson 5 hits are (L to R) Tito, Marlon, Jackie, Michael, Jermaine, and Randy.

EPILOGUE.

ON JUNE 25, 2009, TELEVISION NETWORKS AROUND THE WORLD REPORT BREAKING NEWS. MICHAEL JACKSON HAS
BEEN TRANSPORTED BY AMBULANCE FROM HIS HOME IN THE HOLMBY HILLS SECTION OF LOS ANGELES TO UCLA MEDICAL CENTER.
PARAMEDICS HAVE RESPONDED TO A 9-1-1 EMERGENCY CALL PLACED AT 12:21PM LOCAL TIME. AT 2:26PM, DOCTORS AT
THE MEDICAL CENTER PRONOUNCE MICHAEL DEAD. LESS THAN 20 MINUTES LATER, THE WEBSITE TMZ BREAKS THE STORY
AND SOON AFTER OTHER NEWS SOURCES CONFIRM THE HORRIBLE TRUTH.

THE WORLD MOURNS.

IMMEDIATELY BEFORE his passing, Michael had been rehearsing for a series of fifty concerts, to be held at the O2 Arena in London. The *This Is It* shows were scheduled to begin in July. Instead, a memorial service was held that month at Staples Center in Los Angeles. Michael's family and friends were in attendance, including Berry Gordy, Smokey Robinson, Lionel Richie, the Rev. Jesse Jackson, Mariah Carey, Queen Latifah, Stevie Wonder, Kobe Bryant, Magic Johnson, Brooke Shields, Usher, and two of Martin Luther King's children. The event was broadcast all over the globe, to an estimated one billion viewers.

JACKIE JACKSON: There's never a day that goes by that I don't think about my brother, because he's all around us. The other day, when I was driving down the strip, I was at a stoplight on Las Vegas Boulevard and I turned to the right and there was this big poster of him looking at me. I said, "Hey Mike, what's going on?" Things like that happen all the time. When I walk in a restaurant, or a store, all of a sudden one of his songs will play, so he's around us 24/7 and we miss him dearly. He is always with us in spirit and it will always be that way. We just have to carry on his message, what he was about.

In the liner notes of his solo album *Tito Time*, Tito wrote a tribute to his late brother: "I will never have the words to say how much I miss you.... What I miss the most are just all of us being brothers growing up in Gary and getting into trouble, the practical jokes we all played on people. I promise to keep our legacy alive, always."

In December 2009, the A&E network broadcast the first of six episodes of a reality series, *The Jacksons: A Family Dynasty*. The theme song was the Jackie Jackson/Michael Jackson composition "Can You Feel It," from the *Triumph* album. A&E described the series in a press release: "[It] will chronicle the unscripted lives of...four Jackson brothers—Jackie, Jermaine, Tito and Marlon—as they go about their lives following the death of their brother Michael."

JACKIE: Jermaine came to me and said they wanted to do a reality show. At first, we said no. We never wanted to be on television like that. When they make a reality show, they want some dirt. That's not us. But all the other brothers wanted to do it, and they agreed that they could follow us on tour. I said okay and once

I got into it, I enjoyed it. But Jermaine was always late to the set, because he would peek out to see what we were wearing and then go and change to make sure his outfit was better than ours. That's Jermaine, you know. We had fun doing it, but I've never seen the series, not one episode. I've never watched myself on television.

In June 2012, the surviving members of the Jackson 5 went out on the road for the *Unity* tour. They played seventy dates in thirteen months, and the tour took them all over the world. There were twenty-five dates in North America, but they also played Europe, Asia, Oceania, and Africa. It was the first Jacksons tour without Michael.

JACKIE: It was difficult not having Michael there, not having his presence on stage. During any given song, we knew where he would be on the stage, and we felt him there. So his spirit was always with us. It was a great show and people loved it. We got standing ovations and everybody was dancing. It was very difficult to put the set list together because we've got so many songs. We spent three weeks at my house and at Jermaine's house and Tito's house. It took that long to pick the songs because we tried to choose the songs that the fans loved the most. We had to leave out a lot of songs, and sometimes we would just do a verse and a chorus, then go to the next song because we've got so many. We tried to get in as many songs as possible.

TITO JACKSON: Here's something the world didn't know. Although Michael was doing the O2 Arena, the brothers had already been discussing the possibility of going out again as the Jackson 5/ Jacksons, with Michael. Then the O2 came around and Michael signed to do the *This Is It* tour. He told us that after he did the shows in England, then we could join him as the Jackson 5 and go out and tour again. So that was the plan, for us to join him later at the O2 Arena, maybe do five songs with him, and then go on tour from there. But as we know, that never came to light. Michael passed away and three years later, we put together the *Unity* tour. The fans had been asking us, "When are we going to see you guys again?" People were wondering what the Jacksons were like without Michael. Our family has always been about giving our best. It was good to be on stage again with the brothers.

The Jacksons remain strong as a family, with multiple generations, from Katherine and Joe to their children to their children's children and grandchildren.

JACKIE: When the holidays come around, we all come together and make all kinds of food. You'd be surprised to see how many nieces and nephews there are. Don't ask me how many kids because there are a lot of us. We play basketball and other games and we watch movies. We sing and perform. We do all kinds of crazy things and just have a great time. We eat a lot and friends come by. The Kardashians live across the street, so sometimes they stop by. We have a good time. Our children know the history of their uncles.

It's difficult to believe that fifty years have passed since the Jacksons were driving around in the family's VW van, performing shows and trying to win talent contests. No one could have predicted back in 1967 how it would all turn out—that they would become the music industry's version of royalty, selling records in the multi-millions and spreading their music to every corner of the world. They have made a permanent mark on our culture and will forever be an indelible chapter in the history of humanity.

JACKIE: I've had a great life. I've done everything I've always wanted to do. I'm in the [Rock and Roll] Hall of Fame for what I've achieved. I made music that made people happy around the world. People are still loving that music even today because it was great music with great lyrical content. It wasn't degrading anyone. We made music that brought people together to have fun, dance, and laugh—the kind of music that brought families together at a concert. And still today, youngsters come to our concerts and I say, "Wait a minute. You weren't even around," but they love the songs anyway. They're at the front of the stage, singing our hits. They're like ten or eleven years old and they dress like the Jacksons. So I wouldn't change a thing for all the money in the world.

MARLON JACKSON: It feels good to know that you created music that people appreciate around the world. And that somehow what you've created has affected people's lives in a positive way. As I look back and take myself out of the equation, some of our accomplishments are pretty amazing.

Special Commemorative Edition

TIME

MICHAEL JACKSON
1958-2009

www.time.com

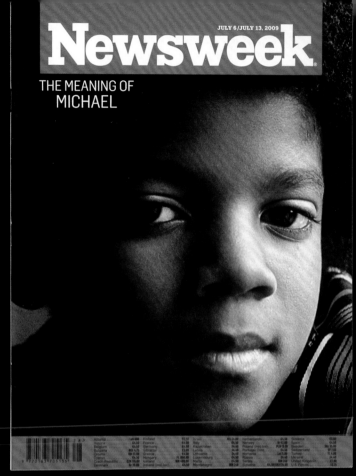

Newsweek

THE MEANING OF
MICHAEL

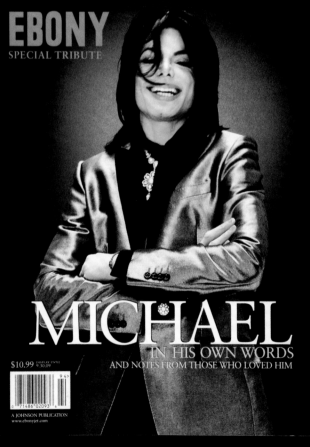

EBONY
SPECIAL TRIBUTE

MICHAEL
IN HIS OWN WORDS
AND NOTES FROM THOSE WHO LOVED HIM

$10.99 DISPLAY UNTIL 9/30/09

A JOHNSON PUBLICATION
www.ebonyjet.com

INT'L BEST-DRESSED POLL · TOM WOLFE: *BONFIRE OF THE VANITIES* 2009

VANITY FAIR

The Style Issue

FEATURING
THE ULTIMATE
MAD MEN
SUMMER-BREAK
ALBUM

Photographs by Annie Leibovitz
Story by Bruce Handy

WHAT'S
RUTH
MADOFF
HIDING?
By MARK SEAL P. 216

Special Collectors' Edition
FAREWELL TO TWO TRAGIC ICONS
FALLEN KING
MICHAEL JACKSON
STUNNING OUTTAKES FROM THE HISTORIC ANNIE LEIBOVITZ DANCE SEQUENCE
Story by Lisa Robinson P. 102

FALLEN ANGEL
FARRAH FAWCETT
THE INSIDE STORY OF HER LAST HEARTBREAKING YEARS
By LESLIE BENNETTS P. 302

September 2009
www.vanityfair.com

"IT WAS A SAD DAY. BUT IT FELT GOOD TO THINK THAT I HAD A BROTHER WHO WAS SO TREMENDOUSLY TALENTED AND WHO TOUCHED—AND CHANGED—THE WORLD. I'M PROUD OF MICHAEL."

MICHAEL JACKSON

AUGUST 29, 1958 - JUNE 25, 2009

"In a world filled with hate,
we must still dare to hope.
In a world filled with anger,
we must still dare to comfort.
In a world filled with despair,
we must still dare to dream.
And in a world filled with distrust,
we must still dare to believe."

MICHAEL JACKSON

We loved him,
We laughed with him,
We sang with him and
We danced with him
But on this day,
We Celebrate Him.

Please join us as we lay
our beloved son,
cherished brother &
devoted father,
Michael Jackson,
in his final resting place.

The Private Service will be held at

Forest Lawn Memorial Park - Glendale
1712 S. Glendale Ave.
Glendale, CA 91205

The Great Mausoleum
Holly Terrace

Thursday, September 3, 2009
7:00 pm

Service will start promptly at 7:00pm

Parking instructions & directions to the Great Mausoleum
will be given at the entrance of Forest Lawn Glendale.

Regrets only by Wednesday, September 2, 2009
818-692-6777

ABOVE This memorial book was given to family, friends, and fans at Michael's memorial service, held at Staples Center in Los Angeles on July 7, 2009. **OPPOSITE** Tickets to the documentary *This Is It* went on sale at L.A. Live in downtown Los Angeles on September 24, 2009. Fans lined up that day to sign a tribute wall for Michael.

MICHAEL JACKSON
AUGUST 29, 1958 – JUNE 25, 2009

ABOVE AND OPPOSITE The 2012–13 *Unity* tour was the first set of live shows that the brothers had performed in three decades and the first since Michael's death. Here, Jackie, Tito, Jermaine, and Marlon are seen rehearsing for the shows (above) and attending a photo session to publicize the tour (opposite). **OVERLEAF** The Jacksons played seventy shows on the worldwide *Unity* tour, beginning in Rama, Canada, on June 20, 2012, and ending in Atlantic City, New Jersey, on July 27, 2013. In an emotional tribute to Michael, Jermaine sang "Gone Too Soon," a song his late brother recorded on his 1991 album *Dangerous*. Bottom right, page 302: the Jackson offspring on stage: [L to R] Michael's son Prince, Jackie's son Siggy, Jermaine's sons Jermajesty and Jaafar, and Michael's daughter Paris.

PREVIOUS In 2015, the four eldest Jackson brothers—Jackie, Tito, Jermaine, and Marlon—performed at Bestival, held at Robin Hill on the Isle of Wight, UK.

OPPOSITE AND ABOVE Along with Duran Duran, the Chemical Brothers, and Missy Elliott, the Jacksons headlined at the DStv Delicious International Food and Music Festival held in Johannesburg, South Africa, on October 9, 2016.

SELECTED DISCOGRAPHY.

US releases only.

PRESENTED TO
JACKIE JACKSON
TO COMMEMORATE WORLDWIDE SALES
OF MORE THAN 200,000,000
ALBUMS SOLD OF
THE JACKSON FIVE
ON
MOTOWN RECORDS

Compilations **C** have been included where they contain previously unreleased material
or where they were released while the band was still signed to the label that released them.

Live albums **L** have been included where they feature material recorded
when the group was still signed to the label that released them.

The symbol ⊕ has been used to indicate singles or albums that were released
in the USA as digital downloads only.

JACKSON FIVE SINGLES

"Big Boy"
January 1968
STEELTOWN RECORDS 45-681

**"We Don't Have To Be Over 21
(To Fall In Love)"** *
1970
STEELTOWN RECORDS 682
–

"I Want You Back"
October 1969
MOTOWN M 1157
#1

"ABC"
February 1970
MOTOWN M1163
#1

"The Love You Save"
May 1970
MOTOWN M 1166
#1

"I'll Be There"
August 1970
MOTOWN M 1171
#1

"Santa Claus Is Coming To Town"
November 1970
MOTOWN M-1174
–

"Mama's Pearl"
January 1971
MOTOWN M 1177
#2

"Never Can Say Goodbye"
March 1971
MOTOWN M 1179
#2

"Maybe Tomorrow"
June 1971
MOTOWN M 1186 F
#20

"Sugar Daddy"
November 1971
MOTOWN M 1194F
#10

"Little Bitty Pretty One"
April 1972
MOTOWN M 1199F
#13

"Lookin' Through The Windows"
June 1972
MOTOWN M 120 5F
#16

"Corner Of The Sky"'
October 1972
MOTOWN M 1214F
#18

"Hallelujah Day"
March 1973
MOTOWN M 1224F
#28

"Get It Together"
August 1973
MOTOWN M 1277F
#28

"Dancing Machine"
February 1974
MOTOWN M 1286F
#2

"Whatever You Got, I Want"
October 1974
MOTOWN M 1308F
#38

"I Am Love (Part I)"
December 1974
MOTOWN M 1310F
#15

**"Forever Came Today"
(A-side)**
June 1975
MOTOWN M 1356F
#60

**"All I Do Is Think Of You"
(B-side)**
November 1975
MOTOWN M 1356F
–

THE JACKSONS SINGLES

"Enjoy Yourself"
October 1976
EPIC/PIR 8-50289
#6

"Show You The Way To Go"
January 1977
EPIC/PIR 8-50350
#28

"Goin' Places"
October 1977
EPIC/PIR 8-50454
#52

"Find Me A Girl"
December 1977
EPIC/PIR 8-50496
–

"Blame It On The Boogie"
October 1978
EPIC/CBS 8-50656
#54

**"Shake Your Body
(Down To The Ground)'**
February 1979
EPIC 8-50656
#7

**"Lovely One"
(Short Version)**
October 1980
EPIC 9-50938
#12

"Heartbreak Hotel"
December 1980
EPIC 19-50959
#22

"Can You Feel It"
March 1981
EPIC 19-01032
#77

"Walk Right Now"
June 1981
EPIC 19-02132
#73

"Working Day And Night"
November 1981
EPIC 14-02720
–

**"State Of Shock"
(with Mick Jagger)**
June 1984
EPIC 34-04503
#3

"Torture"
September 1984
EPIC 34-04575
#17

"Body"
October 1984
EPIC 34-04673
#47

**"We Are The World"
(USA for Africa)**
March 1985
COLUMBIA US7-04839
#1

"Time Out For The Burglar"
March 1987
MCA 53032
–

**"Nothin' (That Compares 2 U)"
(Edited Version)**
January 1989
EPIC 34-68688
#77

**"2300 Jackson Street"
(The Jacksons feat. Michael
Jackson, Janet Jackson, Rebbie
Jackson, and Marlon Jackson)**
July 1989
EPIC 34-69022

* *Recorded while the Jackson 5 were still signed to Steeltown
Records, but not released until 1970, when they had already
gone over to Motown.*

JACKSON FIVE ALBUMS

Diana Ross Presents The Jackson 5
December 1969
MOTOWN MS-700
#5

ABC
May 1970
MOTOWN MS-709
#4

Third Album
September 1970
MOTOWN S-718
#4

Jackson 5 Christmas Album
October 1970
MOTOWN MS 713
–

Maybe Tomorrow
April 1971
MOTOWN MS-735
#11

Goin' Back To Indiana (original TV soundtrack)
September 1971
MOTOWN M 742-L
#16

Greatest Hits
December 1971
MOTOWN MS 741L
#2

Lookin' Through The Windows
May 1972
MOTOWN M 750 L
#7

Skywriter
March 1973
MOTOWN M 761L
#44

G.I.T.: Get It Together
September 1973
MOTOWN M 783V1
#100

Dancing Machine
September 1974
MOTOWN M6-780S1
#16

Moving Violation
May 1975
MOTOWN M6-829S1
#36

Joyful Jukebox Music
May 1976
MOTOWN 865
–

Anthology (3-LP set)
June 1976
MOTOWN 868
#84

Boogie
January 1979
NATURAL RESOURCES 4013
–

In Japan! *
October 2004
HIP-O SELECT B0003070-02
(CD ONLY)

Live At The Forum*
June 2010
HIP-O SELECT/MOTOWN B0014405-02
–

* Featured previously unissued live recordings from 1973, in Osaka. It was originally released in Japan on Tamla Motown SWX-6024 (vinyl version) in 1973. The 2010 release was limited to 5,000 individually numbered copies.

* Featured live recordings from 1970 and 1972.

THE JACKSONS ALBUMS

The Jacksons
November 1976
EPIC/PIR PE 34229
#9

Goin' Places
October 1977
EPIC/PIR JE 34835
#6

Destiny
December 1978
EPIC JE 35552
#11

Triumph
October 1980
EPIC FE 36424
#10

The Jacksons: Live!
November 1981
EPIC KE2 37545
–

Victory
July 1984
EPIC QE 38946
#1

2300 Jackson St
May 1989
EPIC EK 40911
#59

JACKIE JACKSON SINGLES

"Stay"
March 1989
POLYDOR 871 548-7
39

"Cruzin"
(7-inch remix)
June 1989
POLYDOR 889 034-7
#58

"We Know What's Going On"
2010
SIGGIE MUSIC
–

JACKIE JACKSON ALBUMS

Jackie Jackson
October 1973
MOTOWN M 785V1
–

Be The One
September 1989
POLYDOR 422-837 766-1
#84

MARLON JACKSON SINGLES

"Don't Go"
September 1987
CAPITOL B-44047
–

"Baby Tonight"
December 1987
CAPITOL B-44092
–

MARLON JACKSON ALBUM

Baby Tonight
July 1987
CAPITOL CLT-46942
#175

RANDY JACKSON SINGLE

"How Can I Be Sure"
July 1978
EPIC / IVORY TOWER 8-50576
–

JERMAINE JACKSON SINGLES

"That's How Love Goes"
September 1972
MOTOWN M 1201F
#46

"You're In Good Hands"
October 1973
MOTOWN M 1244F
#79

"Daddy's Home"
December 1973
MOTOWN M 1216F
#9

"Let's Be Young Tonight"
September 1976
MOTOWN M 1401F
#55

"You Need To Be Loved"
September 1977
MOTOWN M 1409F
–

"Castles Of Sand"
April 1978
MOTOWN M 1441F
–

"Let's Get Serious"
March 1980
MOTOWN M 1469F
#9

"You Like Me Don't You"
April 1980
MOTOWN M 1503F
#50

"You're Supposed To Keep Your Love For Me"
July 1980
MOTOWN M 1490F
#34

"Little Girl Don't You Worry"
November 1980
MOTOWN M 1499F
–

"I'm Just Too Shy"
October 1981
MOTOWN M 1525F
#60

"Paradise In Your Eyes"
January 1982
MOTOWN 1600MF
–

"Let Me Tickle Your Fancy"
July 1982
MOTOWN 1628MF
#18

"Very Special Part"
October 1982
MOTOWN TMG 1286
–

"Dynamite"
July 1984
ARISTA 1-9190
#15

"Do What You Do"
October 1984
ARISTA AS 1-9279
#13

"When The Rain Begins To Fall" (with Pia Zadora)
January 1985
CURB RECORDS MCA-52521
#54

"(Closest Thing) To Perfect"
June 1985
ARISTA AS 1-9356
#67

"I Think It's Love"
February 1986
ARISTA AS1-9444
#16

"Do You Remember Me?"
July 1986
ARISTA AS1-9502
#71

"Words Into Action"
January 1987
ARISTA AS1-9495
–

"Don't Take It Personal"
October 1989
ARISTA AS1-9875
#64

"Two Ships (In The Night)"
February 1990
ARISTA AS1-9933
–

"I'd Like To Get To Know You"
May 1990
ARISTA AS-2029
–

"You Said, You Said"
October 1991
LAFACE RECORDS 73008-24003-7
–

"I Dream, I Dream"*
April 1992
LAFACE RECORDS 24016
–

* Only available as 12".

JERMAINE JACKSON ALBUMS

Jermaine
July 1972
MOTOWN M 752L
#27

Come Into My Life
May 1973
MOTOWN M 775
#152

My Name Is Jermaine
August 1976
MOTOWN M6-842S1
#164

Feel The Fire
June 1977
MOTOWN M6-888S1
#174

Frontiers
February 1978
MOTOWN M7-898R1
–

Let's Get Serious
March 1980
MOTOWN M7-928R1
#6

Jermaine
October 1980
MOTOWN M8-948M1
#44

I Like Your Style
September 1981
MOTOWN M8-952M1
#86

Let Me Tickle Your Fancy
July 1982
MOTOWN 6017ML
#46

Jermaine Jackson
April 1984
ARISTA AL 8-8203
#19

Precious Moments
February 1986
ARISTA AL8-8277
#46

Don't Take It Personal
August 1989
ARISTA AL8-8493
#115

You Said
October 1991
LAFACE 26001-2

MICHAEL JACKSON SINGLES

"Got To Be There"
October 1971
MOTOWN M 1191F
#4

"Rockin' Robin"
February 1972
MOTOWN M 1197F
#2

"I Wanna Be Where You Are"
May 1972
MOTOWN M 1202F
#16

"Ben"
July 1972
MOTOWN M 1207F
#1

"With A Child's Heart"
April 1973
MOTOWN M 1218F
#50

"We're Almost There"
February 1975
MOTOWN M 1341F
#54

"Just A Little Bit Of You"
April 1975
MOTOWN M 1349F
#23

"You Can't Win (Part 1)"
December 1978
EPIC 8-50654
#81

"Don't Stop 'Til You Get Enough"
July 1979
EPIC 9-50742
#1

"Rock With You"
November 1979
EPIC 9-50797
#1

"Off The Wall"
February 1980
EPIC 9-50838
#10

"She's Out Of My Life"
April 1980
EPIC 9-50871
#10

"One Day In Your Life"
March 1981
MOTOWN M 1512F
#55

"The Girl Is Mine"
(with Paul McCartney)
October 1982
EPIC 34-03288
#2

"Billie Jean"
January 1983
EPIC 34-03509
#1

"Beat It"
March 1983
EPIC 34-03759
#1

"Wanna Be Startin' Somethin'"
May 1983
EPIC 34-03914
#5

"Human Nature"
July 1983
EPIC 34-04026
#7

"P.Y.T. (Pretty Young Thing)"
September 1983
EPIC 34-04165
#10

"Thriller"
January 1984
EPIC 34-04364
#4

"Farewell My Summer Love"
May 1984
MOTOWN 1739 MF
#38

"I Just Can't Stop Loving You"
(with Siedah Garrett)
July 1987
EPIC 34-07253
#1

"Bad"
September 1987
EPIC 34-07418
#1

"Twenty-Five Miles"
October 1987
MOTOWN 1914MF
–

"The Way You Make Me Feel"
November 1987
EPIC 34-07645
#1

"Man In The Mirror"
January 1988
EPIC 34-07668
#1

"Dirty Diana"
April 1988
EPIC 34 07739
#1

"Another Part Of Me"
July 1988
EPIC 34-07962
#11

"Smooth Criminal"
October 1988
EPIC 34-08044
#7

"Will You Be There" (radio edit)
1991
EPIC 34-77060
#7

"Black Or White"
November 1991
EPIC 34-74100
#1

"Remember The Time"
January 1992
EPIC 34-74200
#3

"In The Closet"
April 1992
EPIC 34-74266
#6

"Jam" (feat. Heavy D)
July 1992
EPIC 34-74333
#26

"Heal The World"
November 1992
EPIC 34-74708
#27

"Who Is It"
March 1993
EPIC 34-74406
#14

"Gone Too Soon"
December 1993
EPIC 34-77312
–

"Scream" (with Janet Jackson)
May 1995
EPIC 34 78000
#5

"You Are Not Alone"
August 1995
EPIC 34K 78002
#1

"They Don't Care About Us"
March 1996
EPIC 34 78264
#30

"Blood On The Dance Floor"
March 1997
EPIC 34 78007
#42

"Stranger In Moscow"
August 1997
EPIC 34 78012
#91

"You Rock My World"
August 2001
EPIC 34 79656
#10

"Cry"
December 2001
EPIC 34 79660
–

"One More Chance"
November 2003
EPIC 49K 76802
#83

"Hold My Hand" (with Akon)*
November 2010
EPIC/MJJ MUSIC 88697834032
#39

"Hollywood Tonight"*
February 2011
EPIC 886978808370
–

"Love Never Felt So Good"
May 2014
EPIC/MJJ MUSIC 886978808370
#9

"A Place With No Name"
August 2014
EPIC 88875021182
–

* European CD release pictured. This track was released in the USA as a digital download only.

MICHAEL JACKSON ALBUMS

Got To Be There
January 1972
MOTOWN M 747L
#14

Ben
August 1972
MOTOWN M 755L
#5

Music & Me
April 1973
MOTOWN M 767L
#92

Forever, Michael
January 1975
MOTOWN M6-825S1
#101

The Best Of Michael Jackson
August 1975
MOTOWN M6-851S1
#44

Off The Wall
August 1979
EPIC FE 35745
#3

One Day In Your Life
March 1981
MOTOWN M8-956M1
–

Thriller
November 1982
EPIC QE 38112
#1

**Looking Back To Yesterday:
Never-Before-Released Masters***
February 1986
MOTOWN 5384
–

Bad
September 1987
EPIC E 40600
#1

Dangerous
November 1991
EPIC E2 45400
#1

**HIStory: Past, Present And
Future, Book I**
June 1995
EPIC 474709 1
#1

Invincible
October 2001
EPIC EK 69400
#1

Michael
December 2010
EPIC 88697 66773 2
#3

Xscape
May 2014
EPIC 88843053662
#2

* Six of the album's twelve tracks are credited to the Jackson 5.

TITO JACKSON SINGLES

TITO JACKSON ALBUM

"We Made It"
February 2011
POINT 7 RECORDS
–

**"Get It Baby"
(feat. Big Daddy Kane)**
June 2016
PLAY IT RIGHT MUSIC 19613840
–

"One Way Street"
April 2017
PLAY IT RIGHT MUSIC
–

Tito Time*
December 2016
PLAY IT RIGHT MUSIC SICX 30005
–

* Released as a physical record in Japan, and digitally throughout the world, in 2016. Released as a physical record in the USA in 2017.

313

TOURS & CONCERTS.

THE FIRST US TOUR: 1970

May 2, Spectrum, Philadelphia
June 19, Cow Palace, Daly City
June 20, Forum, Inglewood
Oct 9, Boston Garden, Boston
Oct 10, Cincinnati Gardens, Cincinnati
Oct 11, Mid-South Coliseum, Memphis
Oct 16, Madison Square Garden, New York City
Oct 17, Olympia Stadium, Detroit
Oct 18, International Amphitheatre, Chicago
Nov 28, Rochester Community War Memorial, Rochester
Dec 27, Charlotte Coliseum, Charlotte
Dec 28, Greensboro Coliseum, Greensboro
Dec 29, Nashville Municipal, Nashville
Dec 30, Jacksonville Veterans, Jacksonville

THE SECOND US TOUR: 1971

Jan 2, Miami Beach Auditorium, Miami Beach
Jan 3, Mobile Municipal Auditorium, Mobile
Jan 29, UD Arena, Dayton
Jan 30, Veterans Memorial Auditorium, Columbus
Jan 31, West High School Auditorium, Gary
Mar 27, Hirsch Memorial Coliseum, Shreveport
Mar 28, Municipal Auditorium, New Orleans
Apr 1, Mid-South Coliseum, Memphis
Apr 2, Curtis Hixon Hall, Tampa
Apr 4, Mississippi Coliseum, Jackson
May 28, Spectrum, Philadelphia
May 29, Indiana State Fairgrounds Coliseum, Indianapolis
May 30, Oklahoma State Fair Arena, Oklahoma City
July 16, Madison Square Garden, New York City
July 17, Charleston Civic Center, Charleston
July 18, Hampton Coliseum, Hampton
July 20, Charlotte Coliseum, Charlotte
July 21, Toledo Sports Arena, Toledo
July 23, International Amphitheatre, Chicago
July 24, Cincinnati Gardens, Cincinnati
July 25, Detroit Olympia, Detroit
July 27, IMA Sports Arena, Flint
July 28, Allen County War Memorial Coliseum, Fort Wayne
July 30, Civic Arena, Pittsburgh
July 31, Baltimore Civic Center, Baltimore
Aug 1, Dorton Arena, Raleigh
Aug 2, Macon Coliseum, Macon
Aug 7, Carolina Coliseum, Columbia
Aug 10, Curtis Hixon Hall, Tampa
Aug 11, Birmingham Municipal Auditorium, Birmingham
Aug 13, Municipal Auditorium, Kansas City
Aug 14, Kiel Auditorium, St Louis
Aug 15, Mid-South Coliseum, Memphis

THE THIRD US TOUR: 1971–1972

Aug 29, 1971, Iowa State Fair, Des Moines
Aug 31, 1971, Canadian National Exhibition, Toronto
Sept 9, 1971, Michigan State Fair, Detroit
Sept 12, 1971, Honolulu International Center Arena, Honolulu
Oct 15, 1971, International Theater, Chicago
Dec 27, 1971, Houston Coliseum, Houston
Dec 28, 1971, Memorial Auditorium, Dallas
Dec 29, 1971, Hampton Coliseum, Hampton
Dec 30, 1971, Richmond Coliseum, Richmond
Jan 1, 1972, Municipal Auditorium, Nashville
Jan 2, 1972, Greenville Memorial Auditorium, Greenville
Jan 12, 1972, City Auditorium, Atlanta
Feb 12, 1972, Kiel Auditorium, St Louis
Mar 26, 1972, Hirsch Memorial Coliseum, Shreveport

Mar 27, 1972, Municipal Auditorium, New Orleans
Mar 29, 1972, Curtis Hixon Hall, Tampa
Mar 31, 1972, State Fair Coliseum, Jackson
Apr 1, 1972, Mid-South Coliseum, Memphis
June 30, 1972, Madison Square Garden, New York City
July 1, 1972, Civic Center, Baltimore
July 2, 1972, Coliseum, Norfolk
July 7, 1972, Richmond Coliseum, Richmond
July 8, 1972, Charlotte Coliseum, Charlotte
July 9, 1972, Greensboro Coliseum, Greensboro
July 14, 1972, Cincinnati Gardens, Cincinnati
July 15, 1972, Civic Arena Center, Pittsburgh
July 16, 1972, Public Auditorium, Cleveland
July 18, 1972, International Amphitheatre, Chicago
July 21, 1972, Civic Center, Tulsa
July 22, 1972, Memorial Auditorium, Dallas
July 23, 1972, Houston Coliseum, Houston
July 24, 1972, Municipal Auditorium, New Orleans
July 29, 1972, International Amphitheatre, Chicago
July 30, 1972, International Amphitheatre, Chicago
Aug 4, 1972, Carolina Coliseum Arena, Columbia
Aug 5, 1972, Municipal Auditorium, Atlanta
Aug 6, 1972, Municipal Auditorium, Nashville
Aug 11, 1972, Civic Center, Savannah
Aug 12, 1972, Constitution Hall, Washington, D.C.
Aug 13, 1972, Civic Center, Charleston
Aug 17, 1972, Kentucky State Fair, Louisville
Aug 18, 1972, Municipal Auditorium, Kansas City
Aug 19, 1972, Kiel Auditorium, St Louis
Aug 20, 1972, Indiana State Fair, Indianapolis
Aug 22, 1972, Missouri State Fair, Sedalia
Aug 25, 1972, Cow Palace, Daly City
Aug 26, 1972, Forum, Inglewood
Aug 27, 1972, Sports Arena, San Diego
Aug 29, 1972, Honolulu International Center Arena, Honolulu
Sept 30, 1972, Black PUSH Expo/"Save the Children" Concert, Chicago
Oct 5, 1972, International Amphitheatre, Chicago

THE EUROPEAN TOUR: 1972

Nov 2, Concertgebouw, Amsterdam, Netherlands
Nov 4, Circus Krone, Munich, Germany
Nov 5, Stadthalle Offenbach, Frankfurt, Germany
Nov 6, Olympia, Paris, France
Nov 9, Odeon, Birmingham, UK
Nov 10, Bellevue, Manchester, UK
Nov 11, Empire, Liverpool, UK
Nov 12, Empire Pool, Wembley, London, UK

THE WORLD TOUR: 1973–1975

USA: 1973
Mar 2, Coliseum, Oklahoma City
Mar 3, Coliseum, Monroe
Mar 4, Astrodome, Houston

Japan: 1973
Apr 27, Tokyo Imperial Theatre, Tokyo
Apr 28, Yubin Chokin Hall, Hiroshima
Apr 30, Koseinenkin Hall, Osaka
May 1, Festival Hall, Osaka
May 2, Budokan, Tokyo

USA: 1973
May 5, Coliseum Complex, Portland
May 6, Seattle Center Coliseum, Seattle
May 18, Spectrum, Philadelphia
May 19, Hara Arena, Dayton
May 20, St John Arena, Columbus

Australia and New Zealand: 1973
June 23, Brisbane Festival Hall, Brisbane, Australia
June 26, Festival Hall, Melbourne, Australia
June 29, Beatty Park, Perth, Australia
July 1, Apollo Stadium, Adelaide, Australia
July 2, Hordern Pavilion, Sydney, Australia
July 4, Town Hall, Christchurch, New Zealand
July 5, Athletic Park, Wellington, New Zealand

USA: 1973
July 13, Boston Garden, Boston
July 14, Veterans Memorial Coliseum, New Haven
July 15, Civic Center, Providence
July 17, Hiram Bithorn Stadium, Puerto Rico
July 20, Civic Arena, Pittsburgh
July 21, Pocono State Fair, Long Pond
July 22, Madison Square Garden, New York City
July 24, International Amphitheatre, Chicago
July 25, International Amphitheatre, Chicago
July 28, Olympia Stadium, Detroit
July 29, Saratoga Perfect Arts, Saratoga
Aug 3, Richmond Coliseum, Richmond
Aug 4, Hampton Coliseum, Hampton
Aug 5, Civic Center, Baltimore
Aug 7, Greensboro Coliseum, Greensboro
Aug 8, Municipal Auditorium, Nashville
Aug 10, Carolina Coliseum, Columbia
Aug 11, Omni Coliseum, Atlanta
Aug 12, Convention Center, Miami
Aug 17, Mid-South Coliseum, Memphis
Aug 18, Kiel Auditorium, St Louis
Aug 19, Indiana State Fair, Indianapolis
Aug 21, Municipal Auditorium, New Orleans
Aug 22, Memorial Auditorium, Dallas
Aug 24, Cow Palace, Daly City
Aug 25, Convention Center, Fresno
Aug 26, Forum, Inglewood
Aug 28, Suffolk Downs, Boston

Canada: 1973
Aug 29, Montreal, Quebec (Man and His World)

USA: 1973
Aug 31, Ohio State Fair, Columbus
Sept 2, Honolulu International Center Arena, Honolulu

Senegal: 1974
Feb 1, Demba Diop Stadium, Dakar
Feb 2, Theatre National Daniel Sorano, Dakar
Feb 3, Theatre National Daniel Sorano, Dakar

USA: 1974
Feb 22, Astrodome, Houston

Las Vegas: 1974
(including LaToya, Randy, Janet, and later Rebbie Jackson)
7 Apr, Nevada MGM Grand Hotel, Las Vegas
Apr 9–23 (15 shows)
Aug 21–Sept 3 (4 shows)
Nov 20–Dec 3 (15 shows)

USA: 1974
Apr 26–28, Sahara Tahoe Hotel, Lake Tahoe
May 13, RFK Stadium, Washington, D.C.
June 22, Forum, Inglewood
June 24–30, Mill Run Theater, Chicago
July 8–14, Circle Star Theatre, San Carlos
July 15, Three Rivers Stadium, Pittsburgh
July 16, New Jersey State Fair, Trenton
July 21, Richmond Coliseum, Richmond
July 26, Memorial Auditorium, Buffalo
July 27, Madison Square Garden, New York City

July 29–Aug 4, Front Row Theater, Cleveland
Aug 6, Von Braun Civic Center, Huntsville
Aug 7, Municipal Auditorium, New Orleans
Aug 10, Kiel Auditorium, St Louis
Aug 11, Municipal Auditorium, Kansas City
Aug 16, Civic Center, St Paul
Aug 17, World Expo, Spokane

South America: 1974
Sept 4–Oct 1, including Panama, Venezuela, and Brazil

USA: 1974
Oct 4–6, Sahara Tahoe Hotel, Lake Tahoe

Far East: 1974
Oct 7–Nov 1, including Japan, Hong Kong, Australia,
New Zealand, and the Philippines

USA: 1974
Nov 3, Oakland-Alameda County Coliseum, Oakland

West Indies: January 1975

USA: 1975
Feb 7, Radio City Music Hall, New York City

Jamaica: 1975
Mar 8, National Stadium, Kingston

USA: 1975
June 11, Chicago Stadium, Chicago
July 6, Music Fair, Westbury
Sept 1, Memorial Stadium, Mount Vernon

Mexico: December 1975

THE FINAL TOUR: 1976

Feb 13, Folk Art Theater, Manila
Feb 14, Folk Art Theater, Manila
Feb 15, Folk Art Theater, Manila
Feb 17, Araneta Coliseum, Manila
Feb 18, Araneta Coliseum, Manila
Feb 19, Araneta Coliseum, Manila

THE EUROPEAN TOUR: MAY 19–24, 1977

France, Germany, the Netherlands, and the UK

GOIN' PLACES TOUR: JAN 22–MAY 13, 1978

Including:
Feb 24, Port of Spain, Trinidad
Feb 25, Port of Spain, Trinidad
Feb 26, San Fernando, Trinidad
May 13, Dodger Stadium, Los Angeles

DESTINY WORLD TOUR: 1979–1980

Europe: 1979
Jan 22, Musical Theater, Bremen, Germany
Jan 24, Musical Theater, Bremen, Germany
Jan 26, Musical Theater, Bremen, Germany
Jan 27, Jahrhunderthalle, Frankfurt, Germany
Jan 28, Teatro Monumental, Madrid, Spain
Jan 29, Teatro Monumental, Madrid, Spain
Jan 30, Teatro Monumental, Madrid, Spain
Jan 31, MartiniPlaza, Groningen, Netherlands
Feb 1, Koninklijk Theater Carré, Amsterdam, Netherlands
Feb 2, Koninklijk Theater Carré, Amsterdam, Netherlands
Feb 6, Rainbow Theatre, London, UK
Feb 7, Rainbow Theatre, London, UK
Feb 8, Rainbow Theatre, London, UK
Feb 9, Rainbow Theatre, London, UK
Feb 10, Brighton Centre, Brighton, UK
Feb 11, Preston Guild Hall, Preston, UK
Feb 12, Theatre Royal, Wakefield, UK
Feb 13, Fiesta Nightclub, Sheffield, UK
Feb 15, Victoria Hall, Geneva, Switzerland
Feb 16, Apollo, Glasgow, UK

Feb 17, Manchester Apollo, Manchester, UK
Feb 18, Bingley Hall, Birmingham, UK
Feb 19, Queens Hall, Leeds, UK
Feb 20, De Montfort Hall, Leicester, UK
Feb 21, Sophia Gardens Pavilion, Cardiff, UK
Feb 23, Rainbow Theatre, London, UK
Feb 24, Rainbow Theatre, London, UK
Feb 25, Pavilion Theatre, Bournemouth, UK
Feb 26, Koninklijk Theater Carré, Amsterdam, Netherlands
Feb 29, Théâtre des Carmes, Avignon, France
Mar 2, Le Palace, Paris, France

Africa: 1979
Mar 6, Orlando Stadium, Johannesburg, South Africa
Mar 7, Orlando Stadium, Johannesburg, South Africa
Mar 8, Orlando Stadium, Johannesburg, South Africa
Mar 9, Orlando Stadium, Johannesburg, South Africa
Mar 10, Orlando Stadium, Johannesburg, South Africa
Mar 12, Stade de l'Amitié, Dakar, Senegal
Mar 13, Stade de l'Amitié, Dakar, Senegal
Mar 14, Stade de l'Amitié, Dakar, Senegal
Mar 16, Green Point Stadium, Cape Town, South Africa
Mar 17, Green Point Stadium, Cape Town, South Africa
Mar 19, Orlando Stadium, Johannesburg, South Africa
Mar 20, Orlando Stadium, Johannesburg, South Africa
Mar 21, Orlando Stadium, Johannesburg, South Africa

North America: 1979
Apr 14, Music Hall, Cleveland
Apr 15, Music Hall, Cleveland
Apr 19, Valley Forge Music Fair, Devon
Apr 22, Valley Forge Music Fair, Devon
Apr 25, Arie Crown Theater, Chicago
Apr 26, Arie Crown Theater, Chicago
Apr 27, Arie Crown Theater, Chicago
Apr 29, Arie Crown Theater, Chicago
May 3, Bayfront Center, St Petersburg
May 6, Jacksonville Veterans, Jacksonville
May 10, Houston Music Hall, Houston
May 12, Houston Music Hall, Houston
May 16, Municipal Auditorium, Birmingham
May 17, Municipal Auditorium, Columbus
May 18, War Memorial Auditorium, Nashville
May 19, Atlanta Civic Center, Atlanta
May 20, Orpheum Theatre, Memphis
May 24, Saenger Theatre, Pine Bluff
May 26, Municipal Auditorium, Kansas City
May 27, Oklahoma State Fair Arena, Oklahoma City
May 30, Shreveport Municipal Memorial, Shreveport
June 1, Chrysler Hall, Norfolk
June 3, Township Auditorium, Columbia
June 8, Belk Gymnasium, Charlotte
June 9, Warner Theatre, Washington, D.C.
June 10, War Memorial Auditorium, Greensboro
Oct 2, Municipal Auditorium, New Orleans
Oct 3, Municipal Auditorium, New Orleans
Oct 4, Hirsch Memorial Coliseum, Shreveport
Oct 5, Municipal Auditorium, Mobile
Oct 6, Von Braun Civic Center, Huntsville
Oct 7, Louisville Gardens, Louisville
Oct 12, Spectrum, Philadelphia
Oct 13, Rochester Community War Memorial, Rochester
Oct 14, Civic Arena, Pittsburgh
Oct 15, Saginaw Civic Center, Saginaw
Oct 19, Market Square Arena, Indianapolis
Oct 20, Kiel Auditorium, St Louis
Oct 21, UD Arena, Dayton
Oct 25, Ohio Expo Center Coliseum, Columbus
Oct 26, Onondaga County War Memorial, Syracuse
Oct 27, Memorial Auditorium, Buffalo
Oct 28, Springfield Civic Center, Springfield
Nov 1, Wings Stadium, Kalamazoo
Nov 2, Chicago Stadium, Chicago
Nov 3, Public Auditorium, Cleveland
Nov 4, Cobo Arena, Detroit
Nov 5, Cobo Arena, Detroit
Nov 6, Baltimore Civic Center, Baltimore
Nov 8, Richmond Coliseum, Richmond
Nov 9, Nassau Veterans Memorial Coliseum, Uniondale
Nov 10, Hampton Coliseum, Hampton
Nov 11, Cumberland County Memorial, Fayetteville
Nov 14, Tarrant County Convention Center, Fort Worth
Nov 15, Riverside Arena, Baton Rouge
Nov 16, Mississippi Coliseum, Jackson

Nov 17, Burton Coliseum, Lake Charles
Nov 18, The Summit, Houston
Nov 19, The Summit, Houston
Nov 20, Municipal Auditorium, Columbus
Nov 21, Greenville Memorial Auditorium, Greenville
Nov 22, Savannah Civic Center, Savannah
Nov 23, Macon Coliseum, Macon
Nov 24, Nashville Municipal Auditorium, Nashville
Nov 25, Omni Coliseum, Atlanta
Nov 29, Tingley Coliseum, Albuquerque
Nov 30, McNichols Sports Arena, Denver
Dec 2, Honolulu International Center Arena, Honolulu
Dec 6, Memorial Coliseum, Portland
Dec 8, Seattle Center Coliseum, Seattle
Dec 9, Pacific Coliseum, Vancouver
Dec 13, Swing Auditorium, San Bernardino
Dec 14, Arizona Veterans Memorial Coliseum, Phoenix
Dec 15, San Diego Sports Arena, San Diego
Dec 16, Oakland-Alameda County Coliseum, Oakland
Dec 18, Forum, Inglewood
Dec 21, Haynes Oval, Nassau, Bahamas

North America 1980:
Sept 5, Honolulu International Center Arena, Honolulu
Sept 17–19, Forum, Inglewood
Sept 25–26, Forum, Inglewood

TRIUMPH TOUR: 1981

North America: 1981
July 8, Mid-South Coliseum, Memphis
July 10, MCC Arena, Oklahoma City
July 11, Reunion Arena, Dallas
July 12, The Summit, Houston
July 15, HemisFair Arena, San Antonio
July 17, Riverside Arena, Baton Rouge
July 18, Municipal Auditorium, Mobile
July 24, Greensboro Coliseum, Greensboro
July 25, Charlotte Coliseum, Charlotte
July 26, Hampton Coliseum, Hampton
July 28, Lakeland Civic Center, Lakeland
July 31, Capital Center, Landover
Aug 1, Capital Center, Landover
Aug 2, Memorial Auditorium, Buffalo
Aug 4, Richmond Coliseum, Richmond
Aug 5, Maple Leaf Gardens, Toronto
Aug 7, Nassau Veterans Memorial Coliseum, Uniondale
Aug 8, Riverfront Coliseum, Cincinnati
Aug 9, Richfield Coliseum, Richfield Township
Aug 12, Omni Coliseum, Atlanta
Aug 13, Civic Arena, Pittsburgh
Aug 14, Spectrum, Philadelphia
Aug 15, Hartford Civic Center, Hartford
Aug 16, Providence Civic Center, Providence
Aug 18, Madison Square Garden, New York City
Aug 19, Madison Square Garden, New York City
Aug 21, Joe Louis Arena, Detroit
Aug 22, Market Square Arena, Indianapolis
Aug 23, UD Arena, Dayton
Aug 26, MECCA Arena, Milwaukee
Aug 28, Chicago Stadium, Chicago
Aug 29, Rupp Arena, Lexington
Sept 1, Kemper Arena, Kansas City
Sept 2, Checkerdome, St Louis
Sept 3, McNichols Sports Arena, Denver
Sept 6, Las Vegas Convention Center, Las Vegas
Sept 8, San Diego Sports Arena, San Diego
Sept 10, Cow Palace, Daly City
Sept 15, ASU Activity Center, Tempe
Sept 18, Forum, Inglewood
Sept 19, Forum, Inglewood
Sept 22, Oakland-Alameda County Coliseum Arena, Oakland
Sept 25, Forum, Inglewood
Sept 26, Forum, Inglewood

Cancellations and rescheduled shows
July 19, Lakeland Civic Center, Lakeland
Rescheduled to July 28
July 22, Omni Coliseum, Atlanta
Rescheduled to Aug 12
Aug 8, Spectrum, Philadelphia—Rescheduled to Aug 14
Sept 5, Oakland-Alameda County Coliseum Arena, Oakland
Rescheduled to Sept 22

VICTORY TOUR: 1984

North America
July 6–8, Arrowhead Stadium, Kansas City
July 13–15, Texas Stadium, Irving
July 21–23, Gator Bowl Stadium, Jacksonville
July 29–31, Giants Stadium, East Rutherford
Aug 4–5, Madison Square Garden, New York City
Aug 10–12, Neyland Stadium, Knoxville
Aug 17–19, Pontiac Silverdome, Pontiac
Aug 25–26, New Era Field, Buffalo
Sept 1–2, JFK Stadium, Philadelphia
Sept 7–8, Mile High Stadium, Denver
Sept 17–18, Montreal Olympic Stadium, Montreal
Sept 21–22, RFK Stadium, Washington, D.C.
Sept 28–29, JFK Stadium, Philadelphia
Oct 5–7, CNE Stadium, Toronto
Oct 12–14, Comiskey Park, Chicago
Oct 19–20, Cleveland Municipal Stadium, Cleveland
Oct 26–27, Atlanta-Fulton County Stadium, Atlanta
Nov 2–3, Orange Bowl, Miami
Nov 9–10, Astrodome, Houston
Nov 16–18, BC Place, Vancouver
Nov 30, Dodger Stadium, Los Angeles
Dec 1–2, Dodger Stadium, Los Angeles
Dec 7–9, Dodger Stadium, Los Angeles

Cancellations and rescheduled shows
Sept 3, JFK Stadium, Philadelphia—Rescheduled
   to Sept 28
Oct 5, JFK Stadium, Philadelphia—Rescheduled to Sept 1

Oct 6, JFK Stadium, Philadelphia—Rescheduled to Sept 2
Oct 13, Three Rivers Stadium, Pittsburgh—Moved to Chicago
Oct 14, Three Rivers Stadium, Pittsburgh—Moved to Chicago
Nov 23, Sun Devil Stadium, Phoenix—Cancelled
Nov 24, Sun Devil Stadium, Phoenix—Cancelled

UNITY TOUR: 2012–2013

North America: 2012
June 20, Casino Rama Entertainment Center, Rama
June 22, Star Plaza Theatre, Merrillville
June 23, Fox Theatre, Detroit
June 28, Apollo Theater, New York City
June 29, Borgata Event Center, Atlantic City
June 30, Bergen Performing Arts Center, Englewood
July 1, Modell Performing Arts Center, Baltimore
July 8, Chastain Park Amphitheater, Atlanta
July 17, Hard Rock Hotel & Casino, Albuquerque
July 18, Comerica Theatre, Phoenix
July 20, The Club at Cannery Casino, Las Vegas
July 21, Open Sky Theater, Valley Center
July 22, Greek Theatre, Los Angeles
July 27, Mountain Winery Amphitheatre, Saratoga
July 28, Chinook Winds Showroom, Lincoln City
July 29, Mountain View Plaza, Snoqualmie
Aug 11, Coney Island, New York City
Aug 31, Morongo Ballroom, Cabazon
Oct 12, River Rock Show Theatre, Richmond
Oct 19, Howard Theatre, Washington, D.C.
Oct 20, Beau Rivage Theatre, Biloxi

Europe: 2012
Nov 8–10, Sportpaleis, Antwerp, Belgium
Nov 16–17, Sportpaleis, Antwerp, Belgium
Nov 23–27, Rotterdam Ahoy, Rotterdam, Netherlands

Asia: 2012
Nov 30, du Arena, Abu Dhabi, UAE
Dec 6, Tokyo International Forum, Tokyo, Japan
Dec 7, Tokyo International Forum, Tokyo, Japan
Dec 9, IOCC Event Hall, Osaka, Japan
Dec 12, Palace of the Golden Horses Royal Ballroom,
   Seri Kembangan, Malaysia
Dec 13, Stadium Negara, Kuala Lumpur, Malaysia
Dec 15, Singapore Indoor Stadium, Kallang, Singapore

Europe: 2013
Feb 5, Westfalenhallen, Dortmund, Germany
Feb 6, Jahrhunderthalle, Frankfurt, Germany
Feb 9, Wiener Stadthalle, Vienna, Austria
Feb 11, Atlántico Live, Rome, Italy
Feb 12, Discoteca Alcatraz, Milan, Italy
Feb 17, Ratiopharm Arena, Ulm, Germany
Feb 18, Tempodrom, Berlin, Germany
Feb 20, Falkoner Teatret, Copenhagen, Denmark
Feb 21, Oslo Spektrum, Oslo, Norway
Feb 22, Stockholm Waterfront Congress Centre,
   Stockholm, Sweden
Feb 24, Hartwall Arena, Helsinki, Finland
Feb 26, NIA Academy, Birmingham, UK
Feb 27, O2 Apollo, Manchester, UK
Feb 28, Clyde Auditorium, Glasgow, UK
Mar 2, Pavilion Theatre, Bournemouth, UK
Mar 3, Hammersmith Apollo, London, UK
Mar 5, Olympiahalle, Munich, Germany
Mar 6, Lotto Arena, Antwerp, Belgium
Mar 7, Heineken Music Hall, Amsterdam, Netherlands
Mar 10, Mitsubishi Electric Halle, Düsseldorf, Germany

Australia and New Zealand: 2013
Mar 14, Perth Arena, Perth, Australia
Mar 16, Sydney Entertainment Centre, Sydney, Australia
Mar 17, WIN Entertainment Centre, Wollongong, Australia
Mar 19, Plenary, Melbourne, Australia
Mar 21, Newcastle Civic Theatre, Newcastle, Australia
Mar 24, Riverstage, Brisbane, Australia
Mar 26, Vector Arena, Auckland, New Zealand

Africa: 2013
May 28, OLM Souissi, Rabat, Morocco

North America: 2013
June 30, Staples Center, Los Angeles
July 25, State Theatre, New Brunswick
July 26, NYCB Theatre at Westbury, Westbury
July 27, Borgata Music Box, Atlantic City

Cancellations: 2012
June 18, The Louisville Palace, Louisville
June 19, Riverbend Music Center, Cincinnati
June 24, Fraze Pavilion, Kettering
June 26, Jacobs Pavilion at Nautica, Cleveland
July 3, DAR Constitution Hall, Washington, D.C.
July 6, Time Warner Cable Music Pavilion, Raleigh
July 7, Verizon Wireless Amphitheatre, Charlotte
July 10, Ryman Auditorium, Nashville
July 11, Fox Theatre, St Louis
July 13, Verizon Theatre at Grand Prairie, Grand Prairie
July 14, Bayou Music Center, Houston

UK TOUR 2017: A CELEBRATION OF 50 YEARS

United Kingdom
June 17, Scarborough Open Air Theatre, Scarborough
June 18, Nocturne Live, Blenheim Palace, Oxfordshire
June 24, Glastonbury Festival, Somerset
June 25, Motorpoint Arena, Cardiff
June 30, Newmarket Racecourse, Newmarket
July 1, Love Supreme Festival, East Sussex
July 2, Riverside Museum, Glasgow
July 6, Greenwich Music Time Festival, London
July 7, Haydock Park Racecourse, Liverpool
Aug 25, Blackpool Pleasure Beach, Blackpool
Aug 26, Carfest South, Hampshire

ABOVE The 365-ton stage that Michael designed for the *Victory* tour measured 19,200 square feet and stood eight stories high. It took a convoy of thirty trucks to transport it from city to city.

PICTURE CREDITS.

Every effort has been made to locate and credit copyright holders of the material reproduced in this book. The author and publisher apologize for any omissions or errors, which can be corrected in future editions.

t = top, r = right, l = left, c = centre, b = below, a = above

All material courtesy of the Jacksons unless otherwise indicated.

All archival material photographed by Dan Gottesman © 2017 Jacksons Entertainment unless otherwise indicated.

4–5 Lawrence Schiller / Polaris Communications / Getty Images
15 clb Paul Drinkwater / NBCUniversal Photo Bank via Getty Images
26 Courtesy Adam White. Photo Simon Pask © 2017 Thames & Hudson Ltd, London
27 tr, bl, br Michael Ochs Archives / Getty Images
35 © West Grand Media LLC
36 Pictorial Press Ltd / Alamy Stock Photo
37 bl, br Motown Records Archives
38–39 Lawrence Schiller / Polaris Communications / Getty Images
40 tl, b Courtesy Bettmann / Getty Images. © West Grand Media LLC
40 tr Courtesy Pictorial Press Ltd / Alamy Stock Photo. © West Grand Media LLC
42 Courtesy Adam White. Photo Simon Pask © 2017 Thames & Hudson Ltd, London
46 tl, cl, bl, cr Motown Records Archives
46 br RB / Redferns / Getty Images
47 Courtesy Adam White. Photo Simon Pask © 2017 Thames & Hudson Ltd, London
48–49 Motown Records Archives
50 (both) Courtesy Adam White. Photo Simon Pask © 2017 Thames & Hudson Ltd, London
52 Courtesy AP / Press Association Images. © West Grand Media LLC
54 Motown Records Archives
56 Motown Records Archives
57 (both) Courtesy Adam White. Photo Simon Pask © 2017 Thames & Hudson Ltd, London
58 Courtesy Adam White. Photo Simon Pask © 2017 Thames & Hudson Ltd, London
59 Motown Records Archives
60–61 Library of Congress, Washington, D.C.
64 Courtesy Adam White. Photo Simon Pask © 2017 Thames & Hudson Ltd, London

65, 66-67 John Olson / The LIFE Picture Collection / Getty Images
68 Motown Records Archives
69 Michael Ochs Archives / Getty Images
70 (both) Courtesy Motown Records Archives. © West Grand Media LLC
71 (both) Courtesy Adam White. © West Grand Media LLC. Photo Simon Pask © 2017 Thames & Hudson Ltd, London
72–73 Courtesy CBS / The Jacksons
72–73 Courtesy NBC / The Jacksons
72–73 Courtesy NBC / The Jacksons
72–73 Courtesy CBS / The Jacksons
77–78 © West Grand Media LLC
80–81 © West Grand Media LLC
82–83 (both) Michael Ochs Archives / Getty Images
85, 86 (various) Courtesy Yoann Galiotto, jackson5abc.com
88 Motown Records Archives
89 Courtesy Adam White. Photo Simon Pask © 2017 Thames & Hudson Ltd, London
90–91 (both) Courtesy Adam White. Photo Simon Pask © 2017 Thames & Hudson Ltd, London
92 Motown Records Archives
93 (all) Courtesy Adam White. Photo Simon Pask © 2017 Thames & Hudson Ltd, London
94 Courtesy Adam White. Photo Simon Pask © 2017 Thames & Hudson Ltd, London
95 Motown Records Archives
96 RB / Redferns / Getty Images
97 Courtesy Adam White. Photo Simon Pask © 2017 Thames & Hudson Ltd, London
98–99 Courtesy Adam White. Photo Simon Pask © 2017 Thames & Hudson Ltd, London
100 (all) Robert Abbott Sengstacke / Getty Images
106 (both) David Redfern / Redferns / Getty Images
110 (all) Motown Records Archives
111 (all) Courtesy EMI Group Archive Trust
113 Motown Records Archives
114-115 Gijsbert Hanekroot / Redferns / Getty Images
116 (all) Michael Ochs Archives / Getty Images
118–119 Sam Emerson / Polaris Images
124–125 (all) Michael Ochs Archives / Getty Images
126 Courtesy Adam White. Photo Simon Pask © 2017 Thames & Hudson Ltd, London
127 Michael Ochs Archives / Getty Images
130 (both) Ron Howard / Redferns / Getty Images
131 (both) Frank Carroll / NBCUniversal

Photo Bank via Getty Images
133 tl, tr, cra, clb, crb, bl, br Michael Ochs Archives / Getty Images
133 cla Sankei Archive / Getty Images
140-143 (all) Michael Ochs Archives / Getty Images
146-148 (all) Fin Costello / Redferns / Getty Images
149 (all) Courtesy Adam White. Photo Simon Pask © 2017 Thames & Hudson Ltd, London
151 (both) Fin Costello / Redferns / Getty Images
152-153 Fin Costello / Redferns / Getty Images
155 Richard Pryor / NBCUniversal Photo Bank via Getty Images
162 t, c Michael Ochs Archives / Getty Images
162 b Hulton Archive / Getty Images
164 (both) Courtesy Adam White. Photo Simon Pask © 2017 Thames & Hudson Ltd, London
166 (both), 168-169 Tom Sheehan / Sony Music Archive / Getty Images
170-171 Gijsbert Hanekroot / Redferns / Getty Images
176-177 Rob Verhorst / Redferns / Getty Images
179 David and Dino May
181 b Lynn Goldsmith / Corbis / VCG via Getty Images
184 Lynn Goldsmith / Corbis / VCG via Getty Images
188 Eugene Adebari / Rex / Shutterstock
190-191 Optimus Productions / Rex / Shutterstock
196 © West Grand Media LLC
197 (all) Paul Drinkwater / NBCUniversal Photo Bank via Getty Images
199 Michael Putland / Getty Images
200-201 Sam Emerson / Polaris Images
202-203 Courtesy Entertainment Marketing and Communications International
210 Courtesy Adam White. Photo Simon Pask © 2017 Thames & Hudson Ltd, London
264-265 Sam Emerson / Polaris Images
269, 272, 276 Courtesy Adam White. Photo Simon Pask © 2017 Thames & Hudson Ltd, London
281 Sam Emerson / Polaris Images
287 (both), 292-293 (both) KMazur / WireImage / Getty Images
299 tl, cr David McNew / Getty Images
299 tr Gabriel Bouys / AFP / Getty Images
299 b John Shearer / WireImage / Getty Images

INDEX.

ACKNOWLEDGMENTS.

JACKIE:

I really can't believe how fast 50 years has gone by. What an awesome experience, an incredible great ride we've taken!

I have to give thanks to several people for making this journey safe and sound:

Berry Gordy, Suzanne De Passe, Tony Jones, Hal Davis, Willie Hutch, Walter Yetnikoff, Harrison Funk, Clifton Davis, Deke Richards, Fonce Mizell, Freddy Parent, Kenny Gamble, Leon Hutch;

John McClain, our classmate, seventh brother in the family, for believing and supporting whatever we wanted to achieve;

The wonderful fans we have around the world for their genuine support over the years;

Mom and Dad for putting up with all the loud noise and believing in our talent and success;

And, lastly, to my wife Emily and four beautiful children Siggy, Brandy, River and Jaylen, love you all.

TITO:

I would like to thank, first and foremost, our mother Katherine and father Joe for helping us reach the lights.

To our Sony Music family, we appreciate you taking us to an even greater level.

Thanks also to Dee-Dee for her love.

And to my three sons, 3T, this is my story and a perfect guideline to success!

To you, the fans, thank you for the many years of love and support you've shown us; it is that which motivates me to keep going strong!

MARLON:

I would like to thank the Motown family, in particular Berry Gordy, Diana Ross and Suzanne de Passe, for the opportunities and guidance. My thanks and appreciation also to the Sony Music family.

Thanks also go to my mother and father for providing the foundation that would become the Jackson 5.

To all our fans around the world: we wouldn't be here, doing what we love, were it not for your support through the years.

And to my wife of 42 years, Carol, and my three children, Valencia, Brittny and Marlon Jr., for their love and support.

And last, but not least, it is thanks to our Creator who has blessed this family with a musical gift that we've been lucky enough to share with the world in the hope of uniting it in love.

Study Peace

Fred Bronson:

A book is never written in a vacuum and this one would not have been possible without a wide support network of family and friends, who have been there for me throughout my life. The first person responsible for me writing this book with the Jacksons is long-time friend and colleague Adam White, author of *Motown: The Sound of Young America* (with Barney Ales). It was Adam's book that inspired the Jacksons to make this book happen, and it was Adam who suggested to his publisher that I write this book, not the first time he has done that.

That love of Motown runs deep and has been part of my life from the moment I became a teenager and found employment in a local record store. Thank you, Berry Gordy, and all of the Motown artists, writers and producers for what you created.

This book would not have been completed on deadline if it weren't for the ace researching skills of Brian Carroll, who has lent his expertise to every one of my books as well as most of the television shows I have written over the years.

Working with the Jacksons on this book was a pleasure, and I appreciate the substantial amount of time they gave me to recount their lives. I'm very grateful to Jackie and Emily Jackson, Tito Jackson and Marlon Jackson. I enjoyed all of our interview sessions and your hospitality.

Long before I started writing this book, I appreciated the friendship and support of Harry Weinger and Andy Skurow at Universal Music, not to mention their shared love of everything Motown.

Finally, I feel very lucky to have worked with the great people at Thames & Hudson, starting with Tristan de Lancey, whose support throughout this project has been steadfast and strong. I can't imagine a better team than Jane Laing, Becky Gee, Rose Blackett-Ord, and Rob Dimery. Thank you all for always maintaining standards of excellence.

Fred Bronson has been called "America's foremost chart journalist" by the editor of Billboard *magazine and, as an expert on music, has guest-starred on* American Idol *four times. He has written many television shows, including the* American Music Awards, *as well as shows celebrating the 45th anniversary of Motown, Lionel Richie's country duets album and* Billboard's *Number One Hits. He has also written two episodes of* Star Trek: The Next Generation *and one episode of the animated* Star Trek *series.*

The Jacksons Legacy © 2017 Thames & Hudson Ltd, London

For Picture Credits see p. 317

Front cover photo: Lawrence Schiller / Polaris Communications / Getty Images

Black Dog & Leventhal Publishers
Hachette Book Group
1290 Avenue of the Americas
New York, NY 10104

www.hachettebookgroup.com
www.blackdogandleventhal.com

First published in the United Kingdom in 2017 by Thames & Hudson Ltd, 181A High Holborn, London WC1V 7QX

First American hardcover edition: October 2017

Black Dog & Leventhal Publishers is an imprint of Hachette Books, a division of Hachette Book Group. The Black Dog & Leventhal Publishers name and logo are trademarks of Hachette Book Group, Inc.

Print book designed and illustrated by Steve Russell / aka-designaholic.com

Library of Congress Control Number: 2017943146

ISBNs: 978-0-316-47373-6 (hardcover), 978-0-316-47374-3 (ebook)

Printed in China

10 9 8 7 6 5 4 3 2 1